What Every MOM Needs

Also by Elisa Morgan and Carol Kuykendall

Real Moms
What Every Child Needs
Children Change a Marriage

Elisa Morgan   Carol Kuykendall

What Every MOM Needs

updated Edition

ZONDERVAN®

GRAND RAPIDS, MICHIGAN 49530 USA

MOTHERS OF
MPS.
PRESCHOOLERS
...because mothering matters

ZONDERVAN.COM/
AUTHOR**TRACKER**z

We want to hear from you. Please send your comments about this book to us in care of zreview@zondervan.com. Thank you.

ZONDERVAN®

What Every Mom Needs
Copyright © 1995, 2006 by MOPS International, Inc.

Requests for information should be addressed to:
Zondervan, *Grand Rapids, Michigan 49530*

Library of Congress Cataloging-in-Publication Data

Morgan, Elisa.
    What every mom needs / Elisa Morgan and Carol Kuykendall.
      p. cm.
    Includes bibliographical references.
    ISBN-10: 0-310-27049-9
    ISBN-13: 978-0-310-27049-2
    1. Mothers—Psychology. 2. Mothers—Life skills guides.
    3. Mothers—Religious life. I. Kuykendall, Carol. II. Title.
    HQ759.M863 2006
    646.70085'2—dc22

                                      2006009622

Published in association with the literary agency of Alive Communications, Inc., 7680 Goddard Street, Suite 200, Colorado Springs, CO 80920.

Interior design by Michelle Espinoza

Printed in the United States of America

---

06 07 08 09 10 11 12 • 15 14 13 12 11 10 9 8 7 6 5 4 3 2 1

To you, Mom.
Mothering matters.
And so do you!

Mom, What Do You Need Most?

Me time.
To be loved and appreciated.
A sanity check.
Patience.
Laughter.
A nap.
Freedom from guilt.
Support from my husband.
Adult conversation.
Girlfriend time.
A MOPS group!
To get organized.
Another brain.
Two more arms.
More of me.
Balance.
To know that I'm normal.
To know it'll all work out.
A longer view of life.
Peace.
Hope.

C✸ntents

Acknowledgments

W*hat Every Mom Needs* was first published in 1995, representing twenty-two years of work by women and men in association with MOPS International to understand and address the unique needs of mothers.

After the book had seen ten years in healthy circulation, we decided it was time to scrutinize its continuing relevance — we do this often with the resources we develop at MOPS — and adapt it for the needs of moms today and tomorrow.

It was a big job. We are grateful to the MOPS International Area Coordinators and writer and MOPS friend Jo Kadlecek, who gathered the help of fifty-seven moms in a wide range of demographics of mothers. These moms read the existing book, wrote their comments all over it, and completed a survey. Thank you too to the 770 moms who responded to online surveys regarding their needs. Thank you for giving your time and thought — for taking this research seriously. We're grateful to mom Kristen Kill for her research, and to Jeannette Taylor and Jet Marketing for excellent survey procedures and reports.

Chiefly, we're grateful to Brenda Quinn, freelance writer and mom of three young children, who gathered material old and new and sifted it for her generation of mothers. Brenda carried the bulk of the rewriting responsibility for this project, getting it into a form that we could shape in our voice.

We continue to stand on the shoulders of hundreds of thousands of mothers of preschoolers, volunteers, staff, and board members who have kept MOPS in their hearts. This expanded version would not have been possible without their historical input for this thirty-plus-year-old organization.

And finally, we're grateful for the partnership with Zondervan, and especially the input of Sandy Vander Zicht, and Brian Phipps, and to Rick Christian and Lee Hough of Alive Communications. Thank you for the ongoing opportunity to reach "every mom."

May this book continue to be a resource to launch many moms in their formative years of mothering to be the best moms they can be!

Introduction

Mothering matters . . .
because today makes a difference tomorrow.

MomSpeak

- My dreams and expectations were along the lines of a Pampers commercial—lots of smiles and coos and a perfectly happy and contented baby. Sure, there would be difficult times, but they would not get me down for long. And my love for my baby would overcome any lack of sleep or missed lunches with my girlfriends. Not so, I've learned.

- Being a mom is the hardest, most heart wrenching, most rewarding, and most exhilarating job ever! It's easy to second-guess myself and think I'm not doing a good job. I want to know that there is room for me to "mess up" and know that other moms struggle with the same things.

- After working outside the home for years and supporting myself, staying home with my new baby made me feel like I wasn't "doing" anything, even though I had never worked so hard in my life.

- I need to know that what I'm doing has purpose and is important. I'll wait years before I see any results.

- I need affirmation that the choices I have made are worth it, especially when I cleaned the kitchen floor for the third time that day or stayed home with a sick child.

Camille gazed out the window and watched an airplane make a fuzzy white track through the bright blue sky. *I wonder where it's going*, she mused. *Probably somewhere warm. Somewhere interesting. Somewhere I won't be going for a while! But that's okay.* Her wistful feelings subsided as she glanced at the new photo of the baby. Tomorrow he would turn a year old, and she recently had his picture taken. She couldn't love him more, and she couldn't believe that a year had passed already. How much he had grown. And how much *she* had grown.

This week, it wasn't only little Tucker who celebrated a year. She did too — her first year of motherhood! Her mother had been the one to point it out, and had even insisted on taking Tucker for an entire day so that Camille could have a day to herself to do whatever she wanted.

Today was the day, and Camille had just picked up coffee and returned home. She'd chosen to spend the day here and bring some order to this place where she spent so much time now. Where to start? Dishes filled the sink. There were piles of papers needing attention on one end of the counter and cupboards that needed organizing. The refrigerator needed cleaning, and there was laundry to be done. And the bathroom and bedroom and baby's room ... already she was overwhelmed. It was a familiar feeling these days. She never came close to finishing the to-dos on her list.

Camille wandered to the spare room. She wouldn't spend any time working today, but it would be nice to clean the clutter off her desk. She fingered the paperweight next to her computer. A photo of herself and her work friends on a bench downtown was embedded under a glass dome. *We sure had some fun days together. I miss them.* Working at home wasn't the same. It brought in some needed money and kept her using her brain, but she missed the friendships she'd had at work. She missed what she'd known to be "life as an adult." Now she spent so much time alone with the baby, sometimes she felt like she'd lost herself. Oh, she wouldn't change anything. She was doing exactly what she wanted to be doing — raising a child — and she loved it. But as she reflected on this first year of motherhood, she had to admit that it had brought some challenges she hadn't anticipated.

She glanced at the photos on the wall. Tucker with a cereal bowl on his head and oatmeal all over his face and bib and high chair. Tucker learning to crawl, with toys scattered around the room. Tucker taking a bath. Sweet memories. And then there were the times she *didn't* take pictures. Like when she and Tucker were both horribly sick with the flu and missed the family celebration on Christmas day. The hours and hours spent during the nights, rocking and walking and trying to get Tucker to sleep. The days when getting to the grocery store felt like a major feat. Motherhood was incredibly more consuming than she could have imagined. There had been days she seriously wondered if she was cut out for the job. And days she cringed thinking of the future. She wanted another child or two. But could she handle it? Could her heart handle it? Did she have enough love, enough time, enough confidence? Never had she been more paranoid about strangers and germs and food and accidents, and on and on.

Camille straightened her books and files, and then decided to go to the bedroom. She settled into her unmade bed and pulled a journal from the drawer in the nightstand. The last entry was dated after Tucker's six-month birthday. Yes, *this* was what she needed to do. It had been an amazing year. The year she became a mom! Before doing anything else today, she'd reflect on the year by writing down some of her memories and the thoughts that whirled around inside her soul.

Tomorrow, Tucker turns one, and I celebrate my first anniversary as a mom . . .

The Sweetest Name!

Mama. Mommy. Mom. Mother. However you say it, spell it, or first hear it babbled from your child, the label changes us forever. Remember the first time you filled in "mother" on the form at the doctor's office under "Relationship to patient"? Or the first time your baby uttered, "Mama"? Or your first official Mother's Day celebration?

Magical. Amazing. Endearing. Startling. All of the above! We celebrate mothering. But we're also surprised by it.

Motherhood changes us dramatically. BC — Before Children — we controlled what we did with our daytime hours. Work. Lunch with a girlfriend. Errands. Phone chats. We also took charge of what we did at night — including when we went to bed and how long we stayed there. We said yes or no to invitations to socialize, work out, or shop based on our desires and our schedules. We responded to our husband's sexual overtures and initiated our own — as desired. We were "free" to be.

And then comes Baby. Whether by birth or adoption, that child changes everything!

Our Priorities Are Rearranged

What used to matter *tons* matters less. And what we never even knew mattered at all is now more than a little important.

Suddenly the greatest desire of our heart is not sex with our beloved but sleep. We'd rather go to the grocery store *alone*— and at eight o'clock at night—than wrestle our two-year-old into her jammies. A clean house is a nice idea, but completing a puzzle with our little one somehow seems more important. Everything is turned around.

Our Commitment Is Fierce

Try telling a new mom that her baby will be "fine" for a few hours without her and you'll get a look of disbelief. Moms start out at different places in their attachment, but eventually we're all the same. We are clear that "We're the mom!" and what we sense about our child in terms of her needs, his health, her disposition, his emotions—is accurate. Just *try* to tell us differently! We reign supreme, knowing what we know from a depth of knowing—a mother's intuition. It's a great feeling, this mothering confidence.

But it can also be a little unsettling in a confusing instant when we wonder why the baby is *still* crying or somewhat irritating when our husband or mother-in-law don't seem to "get what we get."

Our Mom-Job Is Hard

As wonderful as our new world is, mothering is also incredibly hard! Harder than anyone told us. As one mom said, "Right after the birth of my first child, I was not emotionally prepared and I didn't know what to expect. What the media portrays (everything is fun and cute and cuddly) is not how it is …"

Just ask the mom who hasn't had a full night's sleep in almost a year, or the mom whose husband travels most of the week, or the single mom with no one to share the load.

Just ask the mother who was on a plane alone with her eight-week-old daughter. "We were stuck on the runway for almost two hours. I lost her pacifier and she screamed for two hours. The flight was packed so I couldn't get up and move around with her."

Mothering is hard, and nothing adequately prepares us for the reality of constantly caring for a totally dependent baby in all circumstances.

Our Needs Shift

Different priorities and a new commitment create a shift in our most basic needs as women—because now we're not just women. We're moms. But hey, moms are grown-ups. Aren't moms "done"? Once we take over the nurturing/developing/teaching/leading/caregiving role, aren't we done with being "under construction" ourselves? A great question—with an answer that is often overlooked.

Just because we've become moms doesn't mean we're finished being children. Or students. Or pilgrims. Moms have continuing needs too. To sleep. To grow. To talk with someone who cares. To regain perspective and find hope.

Let's grab hold of several points regarding needs.

* *Needs are normal.* Every human being has them. Psychologists and social scientists and religious experts agree that all normal people have needs, and healthy people recognize these needs. A mom who believes that

she has no important needs is sure to end up feeling frustrated and empty. Needs are normal at this stage of life, as in every stage of life.

* *Needs are personal.* Some of our needs are greater than others. Your needs may differ from those of your best friend. In some moments, one need may seem much more intense than another, and then they may trade places in importance in the very next hour.

* *Needs must be recognized.* Needs are nagging and insistent. They don't like to be ignored. If they don't receive the attention they demand in a healthy manner, they're apt to rear their heads in undesirable behavior. Psychologist Dr. Larry Crabb reports, "Most psychological symptoms (anxiety, depression, uncontrolled temper, pathological lying, sexual problems, irrational fears, manic highs) are either the direct result of or our defensive attempts to cope with unmet personal needs."[1] Yikes.

Mom-Meet Your Needs and Be a Better Mom!

Sitting through preflight instructions on an airplane, you are told that if the oxygen masks drop down during flight and you are flying with a small child, you should first affix the mask to your own face, and then assist the child. The implication is obvious: You can't help a child to breathe if you've fainted from your own lack of oxygen!

Similarly, moms cannot effectively meet the needs of their children while ignoring their own. And during the days of mothering young children with intense needs, moms must recognize the value of understanding and meeting their own needs, for the sake of their children and families.

Admittedly, this is hard to do. One mom comments, "My husband said that since he did not go to the gym today, he'd like to go on Saturday. I snapped. Was he totally out of his mind? When did our schedule ever dictate time for me to do something for myself? I never leave my children's side 24/7. I love my job as a mom and would not trade it for anything in the world, but I realized that a part of me was dying so that others could live. I had to start taking time for myself, by myself, to be a better mom and wife."

When we learn to recognize and meet our own needs, we'll be better moms. So what are these needs?

Six Needs

In 1995, when we first wrote this book, we surveyed over a thousand mothers of preschoolers about their needs. Their answers came back clear and pointed. They expressed nine specific needs: significance, identity, growth, intimacy, instruction, help, recreation, perspective, and hope.

Ten years later, in surveying a similar bunch of moms, we learn that today's moms are more confident in their mothering. They are better at claiming time for themselves and at recognizing the value of mothering. Having said that, some needs remain, clear and pointed, but a bit different in expression. Today's moms report:

* I need to "stay me" when focusing so much on my child.
* I need to choose carefully because I can't do it all.
* I need to deal with the fears I carry for my children and myself.
* I need hope most. I need hope to get through today. I need hope that my fourteen-month-old son will not kill

himself climbing on everything. I need hope that my son will grow up to be a responsible adult, in spite of my parenting mistakes. I need hope that he will learn what I want to teach him and will take these values to heart. But most of all, I need hope that God will handle everything.

The greatest need reported? Two stand out. Perspective and hope. Moms today want to know how today fits into tomorrow. And they want to know how to hang on when life is so confusing and unpredictable.

Four other needs stand out. Identity: Moms want to know what happened to the other parts of their being when they became mommies. Growth: Moms want to know how to keep developing who they are while they mother. Relationship: Moms want to connect to others in meaningful ways. Help: Moms want help in managing life and everything that comes with children.

Six needs: identity, growth, relationship, help, perspective, and hope. Six needs that when recognized and addressed make us better moms.

Before we launch into these needs, one by one, let's uncover an important truth: Mothering matters.

The Difference That Mothering Makes

In order to truly understand the significance of our mothering, we need to define the worth of mothering. It is not measured by a paycheck or a promotion. Instead, the value of mothering is in knowing that you, and only you, are the mother your child needs. God has chosen *you* for the job. No one else in the world can mean as much to your child as you.

Early childhood is a critical time. In fact, according to some studies, these fleeting years are even more crucial than we once realized. Reports now tell us that a child's environment from birth to age three helps determine brain structure and the ability to learn. One study showed that brain development before age one is rapid and extensive, vulnerable to environmental influence, and lasts for years to come.

Not only is your child's ability to learn affected at an early age, so is her ability to love. A mother's nurturing love builds the foundation of the child's ability to adjust to his or her environment. Speaking at a MOPS International Leadership Convention, child expert and author Jeanne Hendricks said, "To the newborn child, people are everything. The earliest social skill is when that little infant can find and hold the eyes of an adult in what we call the 'quiet-alert' stage. And you never forget it once you've experienced it. It's when that little one looks at you and says, 'Can I trust you?' Because the first developmental task of a newborn child is to find out, 'Is this a safe world? Am I going to be accepted and loved?'"

Along similar lines, other child-development experts tell us that it is secure attachment with the mother that forms the foundation for the child's entire self-structure and identity. A parent and child work together to create an individual who can look in the mirror and squeal with delight, "That's me!" Such a confident declaration grows out of an infant's healthy attachment to mom and becomes the basis for all future relationships.

Writing one hundred years ago, Sigmund Freud described the relationship of a young child to his mother as "unique, without parallel, established unalterably for a whole lifetime as the first and strongest love object and as the prototype of all later love relationships for both sexes."[2] Even earlier, these words appeared in Plato's *Republic*: "You know also that the beginning is the most important part of any work, especially in the care of a young and tender thing; for that is the time at which the character is being formed and the desired impression is more readily taken."

In the adjustment to becoming a mother, we often don't understand the difference our efforts make. But bit by bit, the impact of our lives on those of our children becomes clearer. If we invest ourselves in the formative years when a child is dependent upon parents for his or her development, we will reap the benefits later in life with the joy of living with a more secure and independent child.

Mothering Matters to the World!

While some organizations focus on making a better world for their children, at MOPS International, we put our focus on making better children for our world. Going a step further, we believe that better moms make better children.

Mothering matters not only to the child and to the mother, but also to the world in which they live. As Leo Tolstoy observed in *The Lion and the Honeycomb*, "Yes, women, mothers, in your hands more than in those of anyone else lies the salvation of the world."

Mothering matters. It's one of the most significant undertakings we can ever begin. It shapes our world, our family, and our selves. Whew. No wonder we're tired. No wonder we take it so seriously. No wonder we'd rather do nothing else with our child — than mother. No wonder we care so much and work so hard to do it right.

And no wonder we overlook ourselves in the process.

Here's the empowering, fantastic, and necessary truth on the subject. If we want to be the best moms possible, we'll learn to recognize and meet our own needs — *because mothering matters.*

Six needs. When we learn to recognize these needs in ourselves, they shape who we are and how we mother. Each need has its own chapter in this book, outlining the experience with stories, quotes from regular moms, research, and resources. The Mom Me Times at the end of the chapters lead you to take steps to meet that need. The Mom We Times connect you to other moms in the process of need meeting.

This book is written to every mother of preschoolers — whoever you might be and wherever you might live. Whether you work full-time inside or outside the home. Whether you are married or single. Whatever your heritage or faith. Whether you have three children or one. Whether you are nineteen or forty-two.

Better moms make a better world. We hope this book encourages you to reach your potential in this season of your life!

—Elisa Morgan and Carol Kuykendall
for MOPS International

What Surprised You about Becoming a Mother?

Myself.

My temper and impatience.

How tired I feel.

How much I love my child.

That I could love a second child ... then a third ... as much as my first.

That while I love my children, some days I don't like them.

How I can't wait to get away from my children, and then when I do, how much I miss them.

How being a mom brings out the best and worst in me.

Some things I say to my children that I vowed I'd never say.

How many times a nose needs to be wiped.

How long a day can be.

How quickly children change from stage to stage.

How much more I appreciate my mother.

How much more I understand God's love for me.

How wonderful it is to be called "Mommy."

One

Identity

I Want to Find "Me" Again

*To know me—who I am
and who I am not—is to love me.*

MomSpeak

❋ Who am I? Ha! That's easy, right? I'm a mom. I'm a wife.
I'm a need meeter. I'm a cook. I'm a milk machine. I'm a
Laundromat. I'm tired. I'm ... not sure anymore.

❋ I didn't know I'd have to give up so much of myself.

❋ I'm about 99 percent mom and only 1 percent myself.

❋ My baby takes up all of my day—and all of my self.

❋ I feel strange now when I go out without the kids (which
is rare) ... like I'm not as important alone.

❋ Though I love my children and am proud of them, their
accomplishments are not my report card, nor their short-
falls my failure. I can't wrap my ego around them.

What Every **MOM** Needs

She propped the door open with one hand as she maneuvered the stroller and her three-year-old into the hair salon. "Whew!" Nicole exclaimed as she parked the stroller and began taking coats off both the toddler and the baby. "I made it!" she told the receptionist with a laugh. "I wasn't so sure about an hour ago. I got everybody dressed, and then Jacob spilled Cheerios and milk all over the kitchen floor and himself, and Isabella blew out her diaper. So we had to start all over again. But we're here—and only five minutes late. Not bad!"

The receptionist smiled and paged Tina, who came up front to meet Nicole, still lugging four-month-old Isabella in her infant seat, and big brother, Jacob. "Hey, Jacob! Let's find a special spot for you. You can entertain your little sister while I cut your mom's hair. Okay, buddy?"

Jacob beamed with the recognition of his role as big brother and settled in above his still-strapped-in sister, poking her face and talking to her in cooing tones.

"I'm so glad to be here," Nicole told Tina. "My hair has been driving me nuts. I only hope the kids will hold up for the next fifteen minutes."

"They'll be fine," Tina assured her. "You've got such great kids," she added as she laid Nicole back in the chair to wash her hair.

As Tina lathered her head, the compliment oozed into Nicole's tired muscles like a soothing ointment. They *were* good kids, and she loved them more than life itself.

Rinsed and toweled, Nicole stepped over some toys to the styling chair, where Tina clipped on an apron and then was called to the telephone. "Hang on a minute," she said, spinning Nicole around to face the mirror.

Yeah, that's what I need to do—hang on! But for more than just a minute, Nicole thought. *I need to hang on to myself through these amazing and exhausting days of being a mom!* In the reflection, Nicole could see Jacob playing with Isabella. He clicked his tongue over his baby sister, mimicking his mom. The infant giggled and wriggled in her seat. Nicole smiled and shifted her gaze to her own face in the mirror.

Yikes! she thought. *I should have put on some makeup. But there wasn't time. There never is anymore.* She sighed, staring at her face. When was the last time she'd really *looked* at herself? With her wet hair slicked back from her face, she could see new creases in her forehead. She hardly recognized herself. *Is this what I look like now?* she wondered.

Then suddenly, surprisingly, she felt a strange chill as she saw staring back at her not just a tired mom or an older version of herself—but someone else, someone who looked familiar and yet couldn't be identified. She peered closer. It wasn't so much any particular feature, but the expression, the whole package. And then she knew. Staring back at her from the reflection in the mirror was the face of her mother.

She drew in her breath quickly, checked on Jacob and Isabella, and then took another look in the mirror. *Who are you?* she wondered as she surveyed the face in the mirror. *Who am I anymore? Who's the self I'm trying to hang on to?*

I'm Not Sure Who I Am!

You've probably said it or felt it at least a time or two since becoming a mother, and probably in other stages of life as well. Whether we're twelve or twenty, thirty-two or forty-seven, we keep asking ourselves, "Who am I?" In some stages of life, we embrace the question willingly and engage in a mental wrestling match until we reach a satisfying answer. But for the mother of young children, the question can seem a bit threatening. All tangled up with our roles and responsibilities, the answer is elusive.

As new mothers, whether we realize it or not, we need to redefine ourselves. We need to find and accept the kind of definition that will keep us going and keep us content during this season when we're both ecstatic to be answering to "Mommy" for the first time, yet we're also pulled and stretched and drained and sometimes overwhelmed by the responsibility of taking care of kids, and others too. Though most of us are treasuring these days of raising children and being a mother, we're like Nicole, who was suddenly confronted with the question that all new mothers inevitably ask, "Who am I *now*?"

Who Am I?

As moms we tend to define ourselves most easily in terms of our external circumstances. We look in the mirror, and instead of seeing our reflection as an identity in its own right, we see the various facets of our life staring back at us.

I Am What I Do

When we go to a school event or meet a new neighbor who asks, "What do you do?" we women are likely to label ourselves in terms of a relationship or a job description — "I'm Madison's mom"; "I'm Ryan's wife"; "I'm a paralegal"; "I'm a part-time consultant"; "I'm in human resources management." (That last one might just fit every mom!)

For moms who have taken time off work to be at home with their children, this common icebreaker often causes us to cringe. *Do I respond with what I used to do, before kids?* And then we engage in the mental wrestling match of wanting others to see the bigger picture of ourselves, yet insisting that what we're doing now — mothering — is of utmost significance and is enough of an identity for now.

Those of us who are working, whether at home or outside the home, may struggle too. We're wearing countless hats every day, and trying to summarize what we do in a meaningful and accurate sentence feels like a huge injustice to all of our roles.

I Am What Others Need Me to Be

This season of life is a season of self-sacrifice, but as moms, we often lose our identities as we're swept into the role of being a need meeter.

We can't help but feeling sometimes that we cease to exist for anything other than meeting the needs of others, and we not only begin to identify ourselves in that way, but we begin to measure our value and worth by our ability to meet those needs. If my baby is good (sleeps through the night, learns to crawl or walk on schedule, interacts well with other children), then I tell myself that I have met his needs and I am good. If my baby is bad (screams when I leave the room, hits other children, or flushes my watch down the toilet), then I accuse myself of not meeting her needs and I am bad.

For those of us who are married, meeting the needs of a husband can also preempt our own identities. We are the ones who support a husband through challenges at work and employment transitions. We're often the caretaker who makes sure he has clean shirts and socks. We advise him in his interactions with the children, and we may serve as his only close friend and confidante. As we focus so much of ourselves on him, our identity can come to feel like simply an extension of his. Or he can seem less like a life partner and more like another child. As one mom confesses, "My husband set up an elaborate plan to appreciate his employees, and I feel left out."

While this may sound like an oversimplification, we often do get our identities confused with the role of need meeter.

I Am What I Accomplish

Many of us believe that who we are equals what we accomplish. "I'm a painter; here are my pictures." Or, "I'm an accountant; here is my database of clients." We are validated by the results of our efforts. In a stage of life where we may accomplish little more than getting to the grocery store or keeping up with the dirty dishes and diapers, an identity based on accomplishment is an identity at risk. Even if we are working full- or part-time, we often feel incapable of accomplishing all we need to do at our job. Something always seems to be left undone.

I Am What I've Experienced

Another partial picture of identity is taken from the past. From the time we feed as infants in our own mother's arms and focus on her eyes, only inches from our own, we are drinking in messages about who we are. She becomes the mirror that gives us our identity. In her praise and criticism, patience and impatience, approval and disapproval, we develop an image of who we are. So too with our father. For those who had a father in the house, he came home from work and lifted us in the air, mirroring back to us how important we were to him. Or he brushed us aside to concentrate on the television, or more work at home, and we concluded that we are of no value at all.

Siblings and our birth order among them in the family describe our place in the scheme of life. As firstborns, we often see a reflection of superiority in our first-place rankings. As second borns, we see competition and conditional love in the eyes of the one above us. Opposite-sex siblings challenge our sexual identity, while same-sex siblings underline it. And those of us who experienced some trauma in our past often live with wounded identities in the present. We moms are like a whirling mirror ball suspended from the ceiling of a dance floor. The painful past scatters the shards of broken images, leaving us unsure of who we were, who we are, and who we will become.

Yet all of these mirrors offer only pieces of our identity. Even the combination of our responsibilities, our activities, and our past isn't enough. Who we are is larger than any one of these and more than their combination. Yes, we're much more than a collection of mirrors, moms!

Who Am I *Not?*

While the mirrors around us reflect an incomplete picture of identity, they can also offer inaccurate reflections, confusing our understanding of who we are. Those pieces of glass may hold some downright lies about us! Actress and author Nancy Stafford writes, "For too long we've been looking in the wrong mirror. We've been seeing ourselves the way others see us, not the way God sees us. It's just like looking in a mirror at a funhouse. When we look at others to see who we are, we get a distorted view, and when we act as if the image is true, we're deceived."[1]

To understand who we are, moms, we have to come to grips with who we are *not*.

I Am Not My Children!

In this season of constant giving, when our children are nearly totally dependent upon us, we derive some sense of value from their responses and accomplishments, but the lines separating us can grow fuzzy. We have to remind ourselves that we are separate. The goal of our role as mothers, in fact, is to continually strengthen that separateness. As psychologist Erik Fromm writes, "In motherly love, two people who were one become separate."[2]

I Am Not My Mother!

Much as many of us love our mothers, perhaps one of the greatest shocks of mothering is looking at ourselves and seeing the traits of our own mothers. When we become mothers, we're mentally thrown back to our own childhood. We think about the positives and negatives of our own upbringing. We think about our mothers and the way they mothered us. We begin to identify with the choices they made, the struggles they had, and the cost they paid in being our moms.

It's good for us to reflect on the past and on what our own mothers brought to parenting. We can't escape the influence they've had on us and on how we will parent and who we will be as mothers and women. Yes, each of us possesses some of the qualities of our own mothers. But, at the same time, each of us is unique. A pivotal truth is that "similar to" does not mean "the same as." While you may have inherited your mother's bone structure, you do not necessarily have her temper. While you may have picked up a creative streak from her, you don't have to repeat her habit of negative nagging.

You may be like your mother in some ways, but you are *not* your mother. Nor are you your mother-in-law, your grandmother, or your stepmother.

I Am Not My Sister, My Neighbor, or Any Other Woman!

Sure, your older sister has this mothering thing down pat. She's been at it for eight years longer than you have. And your super-mom neighbor probably just *looks* like she knows what she's doing. But I'll bet that beneath her up-to-date clothes and well-maintained house or apartment, she still struggles with some aspect of her day. Don't let her fool you.

We all have plenty of room for improvement, and when we let comparisons determine our personal worth, we're using the wrong measuring stick! Your value is not dependent upon how you stack up next to someone else. You are not your sister, your neighbor, or anyone else you admire.

So Who Am I Really?

If you're more than the sum of your responsibilities and relationships, your accomplishments and your past, and you know who you are not, then who are you, really? The question still begs an answer, which may not be discovered quickly. As one mom said, after moving to a new town near her in-laws, with a two-year-old and a new baby, "I needed time to myself ... to get to know me as the mother of two, the daughter-in-law, and

What Every **MOM** Needs

the new friend, while still growing my relationship with my husband. I needed space to find my groove, I guess."

The true answer to the "who am I" question is simpler, greater, and more enduring than all these partial or inaccurate reflections. And it may take longer to understand or believe.

Our true identity comes not from looking into horizontal mirrors—at reflections of ourselves or our mothers or our past—but looking up at God. As we come to understand the truth of who he is, we begin to get a true picture of ourselves. Know why? He created us in his image.

Nancy Stafford explains, "You will find [your identity] in the pages of an ancient Book, where the Creator of the universe tells you over and over again who you really are, how valuable you are to Him, and how much He loves you and accepts you. Only through the pages of the Book can you discover who you are. . . . The Bible is full of God's opinion of you."[3]

Our goal as moms is to know our true identity in God's eyes, because the Bible promises that the truth will set us free (John 8:32). The truth will ground us as we juggle our roles and will free us to carry on in a culture that too often doesn't appreciate all we are in fulfilling this life as mothers. Three foundational truths tell us who we are.

I Am Unique

You are *you*—a unique combination of personality traits, physical makeup, talents, and abilities. Think about it—you are either an extrovert or an introvert, a morning or night person, type A or B on the stress scale, small- or large-boned; the list goes on. Others may have similar traits, but no one is

packaged exactly like you. God has created you uniquely ...
to be who you are.

As moms, we're quick to recognize the uniqueness of our children. No two siblings are exactly alike, and often they seem like polar opposites. Though both are brought up in the same environment, one may be strong-willed while the other is compliant. One loves all foods; the other is picky. Yet are we as quick to acknowledge and accept our own uniqueness?

Renowned choreographer Agnes de Mille once told fellow dancer Martha Graham,

> There is a vitality, a life force, and energy, a quickening that is translated through you into action, and because there is only one of you in all of time, this expression is unique. And if you block it, it will never exist through any other medium and [it will] be lost. The world will not have it. It is not your business to determine how good it is nor how valuable nor how it compares with other expressions. It is your business to keep it yours clearly and directly.[4]

You are unique!

I Am Imperfect

Each of us, no matter how hard we try, falls short of perfection, and this imperfection is most often revealed within the context of our close relationships. We try to be good mothers, but sometimes what we see surprises — and disappoints — us.

"Indeed, the struggle of self-acceptance is, in a strong sense, a case of disillusionment," writes Martha Thatcher. "We may be disappointed in our character, our abilities, or our role in life; we had thought it would all be quite different. No matter how many good points about ourselves we become aware of, we are still disappointed in what is not there."[5]

What we discover in our most intimate relationships is that we are not perfect, but the comforting truth is that God is the first one we can run to, imperfections and all. Jesus chose to spend most of his time with people who had obvious imperfections, and he showed the most anger toward those people who acted as if they had it all together. God asks that we see ourselves for who we really are, admitting to our weaknesses.

Coming to grips with who we are doesn't mean that we wallow in our imperfections. But coming to see ourselves in truth requires that we take off any masks of denial and admit our inadequacies. They too help us define ourselves.

Psychologist Cecil Osborne writes, "The people I know who truly like themselves as persons, apart from their roles in life as husband, wife, parent, or job-holder, are those who have learned to be honest with themselves and who to some degree understand themselves."[6]

Yes, we're imperfect. Much as we love our kids, much as we intend to be the best moms we can be, we are fallible human beings who are in process. We will make mistakes; we will lose our patience; we will sometimes act unlovingly.

I Am Loved

God loves us unconditionally—without regard to our performance or goodness or consistent ability to be good mothers. The whole Bible is God's love story to us.

Pondering this concept of God's unconditional love, or grace, author Philip Yancey writes, "Grace means there is nothing I can do to make God love me more, and nothing I can do to make God love me less."[7]

It's true. Whether or not your mother loved you, your child gets angry at you, or your husband says "I love you" often enough, the truth is, you are loved, and nothing you do will ever change that.

Getting to Know Me

Learning to apply these truths in our lives as mothers of young children is a process. In a simple checklist, here's what these truths mean:

* *We need to know ourselves the way God knows us.* If we know ourselves — recognizing our uniqueness and our imperfections — and know that God loves us, we are free to accept ourselves. We are even free to love ourselves. God tells us to love our neighbors *as ourselves* (Matthew 22:39). This is not a prideful type of self-love. Rather, it's a secure acceptance of ourselves. It is seeing ourselves as God sees us. This is our true identity, which sets us free from guilt and self-consciousness and put-downs. This self-acceptance meets a critical need that moms have.

* *We need to care for ourselves for the sake of our children.* We are our children's most significant role models. From us they learn and internalize how to live life in this world. The healthier we are and become physically, emotionally, relationally, and spiritually, the healthier they are likely to become as they grow.

   Like the feel-good endorphins released in your body during physical exercise, taking care of yourself helps you take better care of others, in spite of the trade-offs. As an active MOPS leader says, "Sometimes take-out dinners and an extra night of babysitting are a fair price for a self-confident mommy who is sure of her gifts and able to pass the 'endorphins' of her leadership on to her family."[8]

When we take care of ourselves, we are, most definitely, taking care of our children. Granted, it takes extra energy and planning to fit self-care into your days, but if you do, everyone will benefit. So don't stop working on yourself, Mom.

* *We need to accept ourselves for the sake of our children.* There is a lot of talk these days about how to boost a child's self-esteem. If we step back and think about it, the most logical way to nurture a child's self-esteem is to model what it means to accept ourselves, with all our quirks, idiosyncrasies, passions, strengths, and weaknesses. If we're committed to continuing to grow and change, the best way to help a child love himself or herself is to live a life in which we love and accept ourselves. Remember, kids have an uncanny way of sensing the unspoken, and even if they can't put it in words, they know when their parents don't like themselves. If you need to, *work* at learning to like yourself!

* *We need to accept ourselves for the sake of others around us.* Even the Golden Rule tells us to love our neighbor *as ourselves.* The very core of the rule requires that we love *ourselves.* If we don't, we're unable to truly love others! It's as simple as that.

Who am I? The question keeps popping up as we grow and change. Which mirror gives the truest answer, the one that will sustain us through changing circumstances and changing roles? Horizontal mirrors will help you to know parts of yourself as you look to your family and your past for answers. But it is the vertical mirror—what we see when we look at God—that gives us the truest reflection of ourselves. God reminds us who we are. He tells us the truth that sets us free to know ourselves, to accept ourselves, and to be ourselves.

Mom Me Time

Mom Me Time 1
Understand Your Personality!

As moms, part of affirming our own identity is discovering or reminding ourselves who God uniquely created us to be. Understanding our individual personality gives us the tools we need as mothers and as women to overcome our natural weaknesses, find freedom to live in our strengths, and understand that each personality has its own set of emotional needs. Meeting these emotional needs in proper ways is the key to keeping ourselves healthy for our families and for ourselves.

In the following personality profile, circle a word from each line that best describes you. Add up your total number of answers in each of the four columns, and add your totals from both the strengths and weaknesses sections together. You will find your dominant personality type. You'll also know what combination of personalities you are. If, for example, your score is 35 in Powerful Choleric strengths and weaknesses, there's really little question. You're almost all Powerful Choleric. But if your score is, for example, 16 in Powerful Choleric,

14 in Perfect Melancholy, and 5 in each of the others, you're a Powerful Choleric with a strong Perfect Melancholy. You'll also know your least dominant type.[9]

STRENGTHS

Popular Sanguine	Powerful Choleric	Perfect Melancholy	Peaceful Phlegmatic
Animated	Adventurous	Analytical	Adaptable
Playful	Persuasive	Persistent	Peaceful
Sociable	Strong-willed	Self-sacrificing	Submissive
Convincing	Competitive	Considerate	Controlled
Refreshing	Resourceful	Respectful	Reserved
Spirited	Self-reliant	Sensitive	Satisfied
Promoter	Positive	Planner	Patient
Spontaneous	Sure	Scheduled	Shy
Optimistic	Outspoken	Orderly	Obliging
Funny	Forceful	Faithful	Friendly
Delightful	Daring	Detailed	Diplomatic
Cheerful	Confident	Cultured	Consistent
Inspiring	Independent	Idealistic	Inoffensive
Demonstrative	Decisive	Deep	Dry humor
Mixes easily	Mover	Musical	Mediator
Talker	Tenacious	Thoughtful	Tolerant
Lively	Leader	Loyal	Listener
Cute	Chief	Chartmaker	Contented
Popular	Productive	Perfectionist	Pleasant
Bouncy	Bold	Behaved	Balanced

Strengths Totals

_____   _____   _____   _____

WEAKNESSES

Popular Sanguine	Powerful Choleric	Perfect Melancholy	Peaceful Phlegmatic
Brassy	Bossy	Bashful	Blank
Undisciplined	Unsympathetic	Unforgiving	Unenthusiastic
Repetitious	Resistant	Resentful	Reticent
Forgetful	Frank	Fussy	Fearful
Interrupts	Impatient	Insecure	Indecisive
Unpredictable	Unaffectionate	Unpopular	Uninvolved
Haphazard	Headstrong	Hard to please	Hesitant
Permissive	Proud	Pessimistic	Plain
Angered easily	Argumentative	Alienated	Aimless
Naive	Nervy	Negative attitude	Nonchalant
Wants credit	Workaholic	Withdrawn	Worrier
Talkative	Tactless	Too sensitive	Timid
Disorganized	Domineering	Depressed	Doubtful
Inconsistent	Intolerant	Introvert	Indifferent
Messy	Manipulative	Moody	Mumbles
Show-off	Stubborn	Skeptical	Slow
Loud	Lord over others	Loner	Lazy
Scatterbrained	Short-tempered	Suspicious	Sluggish
Restless	Rash	Revengeful	Reluctant
Changeable	Crafty	Critical	Compromising

Weaknesses Totals

_____   _____   _____   _____

Combined Totals

_____   _____   _____   _____

What Every **MOM** Needs

By understanding ourselves better, we gain insight into the kind of mother we are becoming, as well as the kind of friend and spouse we are. A better understanding of personalities also helps us understand our children, spouse, friends, and extended family better.

We each have certain emotional needs as mothers because of our personalities. A Sanguine mom needs to have regular doses of fun and lots of interaction with people who like her. A Melancholy mom, on the other hand, needs regular periods of quiet and interaction with others who think deeply and sensitively. A Choleric mom needs to have some areas in her life where she is in control and can see her accomplishment. And a Phlegmatic mom needs regular time with family or friends where conflict is absent and she doesn't have to be in charge. It's inevitable that as moms of young children, we'll find our primary emotional needs are challenged and often unmet in the course of a regular day. But we can't let our needs go unmet indefinitely. If we do, we will suffer, and our mothering will suffer as well. Know yourself and remember who you are. Meeting your needs isn't selfish. It's as essential as our need for the air we breathe and the food we eat!

Loving our families and the others in our lives will take on new meaning, as well, when we understand that we need to show love in the particular ways they are wired to need love. We will naturally love our families in the way we personally want to be loved, but if children or a spouse have different personalities, we may need to step outside our natural inclinations and love them in ways that particularly fit them.

Keep seeking to better understand yourself and your family. Everyone will be happier!

Mom Me Time 2
Find Your Purpose

In her book *Designing a Woman's Life*, author Judith Couchman says, "When we dare to claim our uniqueness and consider what delights us (without feeling unworthy or guilty about it), we step closer to becoming our authentic selves rather than who others tell us to be."[10] She encourages women to get to know their uniqueness and then to discover their life purpose. "When we set out to discover a life purpose, we embark on a journey within, for to understand our reason for being is to recognize the shape of our souls."[11]

What is your life purpose? Who are you, uniquely, and what is your overarching purpose for life? Judith gives these examples of a life purpose statement:

To compose music that draws people to the beauty in God's soul.

To help people eat healthily, freeing them to live as God's temples.

To manage finances so families and companies align with biblical principles regarding money.[12]

To begin your own journey of discovering your life purpose and writing a life purpose statement, spend time writing in a journal using the following questions:

1. If I could spend a day (eight hours), with or without my family, doing anything, what would I do?
2. What are my talents?
3. What are my dreams?
4. What stirs my passion?

5. What is my calling?
6. Can I pursue this purpose now, even as I live as a mother to young children? How?
7. How can my mothering enhance my growth in fulfilling my purpose?

Mom Me Time 3
Pray

Repeat this prayer of acceptance:

Today, O Lord, I accept your acceptance of me.
I confess that you are always with me and always for me.
I receive into my spirit your grace, your mercy, your care.
I rest in your love, O Lord, I rest in your love. Amen.[13]

Mom Me Time 4
Come out of Hiding!

In their book *Captivating: Unveiling the Mystery of a Woman's Soul*, authors John and Stasi Eldredge write, "To live as an authentic, ransomed, and redeemed woman means to be real and present in this moment. If we continue to hide, much will be lost. We cannot have intimacy with God or anyone else if we stay hidden and offer only who we think we ought to be or what we believe is wanted.... *You have only one life to live. It would be best to live your own.*"[14]

Consider what causes you to hide. Do any of the following statements ring true for you?

❋ I am hiding by acting like the girl my father/mother has always expected me to be.

* I am hiding by trying to be the kind of woman my husband wants me to be.
* I am hiding by trying to stay in line with the kind of woman I think my kids will want to remember me as. I don't want my kids to grow up wishing for another kind of mom.
* I am hiding by constantly trying to be a composite of many women I see around me — usually women who have skills I lack or personalities different from mine.
* I am hiding by agreeing to fit nicely into the roles I feel are acceptable in my church and social community.
* I'm hiding behind what I feel are cultural norms ascribed to women and mothers. I'm not sure I have the courage to buck the tide.
* I am hiding behind my own fears. I'm afraid of failing, or looking stupid, or being rejected if I reach for my dreams and let my latent true self emerge.

Spend some time thinking more deeply about what makes you hide who you really are. You may want to journal your thoughts. Can you confide in your husband or a friend as you explore these identity questions? Consider asking for God's help in coming out of hiding and being in fullness the woman and mother he has created you to be.

Mom Me Time 5
Recognize When You Need Help

In taking these steps toward self-acceptance, some people bog down in the negative messages of their past and need more help than a husband or relative or friend can offer. Here are some warning signals that—if they persist—might mean you should turn to a pastor, a caring woman in leadership at your church or a local church, or a professional counselor for help:

* Persistent sad, anxious, or "empty" mood
* Feelings of hopelessness or pessimism
* Feelings of guilt, worthlessness, or helplessness
* Insomnia, early-morning awakening, or oversleeping
* Loss of appetite or weight loss or both—or overeating and weight gain
* Decreased energy, fatigue, a feeling of being "slowed down"
* Thoughts of death or suicide; attempts at suicide
* Restlessness or irritability
* Difficulty concentrating, remembering things, or making decisions
* Persistent physical symptoms such as headaches, digestive disorders, and chronic pain
* Difficulty in giving adequate, consistent care to your children
* Fears that you may harm your child

Please don't hesitate to seek outside help! Most of us need this kind of help sometime in our lives. It is the best thing you can do for yourself if you are hurting in these ways.

Mom We Time

If you are able to read this book with one or more moms and talk about it together, please do! Following are a few questions to get you started in your discussion of the chapter.

1. Can you identify with the kind of "identity crisis" this chapter discusses and many mothers of young children experience? When did you first begin sensing a loss of identity? What challenges are you experiencing now as you consider your identity as a woman, a mother, a wife, and a person?

2. Where do you struggle most in believing untruths about who you are? Which of the following discussed in this chapter tends to threaten you most:

- ❏ *I am what I do:* I can't get past this feeling that I should have some title, some proof that I'm accomplishing something valuable, even though I know in my heart that caring for my children is extremely valuable.
- ❏ *I am what others need me to be:* I'm so concerned about failing my kids or my husband or my employer that I've become consumed with meeting their needs. I rarely get past the routine to think a creative thought or do something spontaneous.
- ❏ *I am what I accomplish:* I have long "to-do" lists every day and spend my waking hours carrying out my list — and some of my nighttime hours thinking about tomorrow's to-dos!
- ❏ *I am what I've experienced:* I feel like I'm in bondage to my own upbringing. It was so flawed that I'm constantly working to make sure things are different for my children. I wonder if I'm pushing it too far and making my kids, and myself, crazy.

3. What do you most need to do to get to know yourself better? Discuss together.

* Take more time out for myself. I need some time for me!
* Learn more about how God feels about me. I need to make time for God in my life.
* Get a handle on my emotions.
* Do some reading and get intentional about uncovering the real me.
* Get some professional therapy. I'm finally believing that it's the healthy people who seek therapy.
* Begin to journal my thoughts, dreams, and discoveries about myself.

For Further Reading

Books

Couchman, Judith. *Designing a Woman's Life: Discovering Your Unique Purpose and Passion* (also available in a Bible study and workbook format).

Eldredge, John. *Waking the Dead: The Glory of a Heart Fully Alive.*

Eldredge, John, and Stasi Eldredge. *Captivating: Unveiling the Mystery of a Woman's Soul.*

Goyer, Tricia. *Life Interrupted: The Scoop on Being a Young Mom.*

Higgs, Liz Curtis. *Mirror, Mirror on the Wall, Have I Got News for You! An A to Z Faith Lift for Your Sagging Self-Esteem.*

Jarrell, Jane. *Secrets of a Mid-Life Mom.*

Leman, Kevin. *The Birth Order Book: Why You Are the Way You Are.*

————. *First-Time Mom: Getting Off on the Right Foot; from Birth to First Grad.*

Littauer, Florence. *Personality Plus: How to Understand Others by Understanding Yourself.*

Littauer, Marita, and Florence Littauer. *Wired That Way: The Comprehensive Personality Plan.*

Rinehart, Paula. *Strong Women, Soft Hearts: A Woman's Guide to Cultivating a Wise Heart and a Passionate Life.*

Stafford, Nancy. *Beauty by the Book: Seeing Yourself as God Sees You.*

Thomas, Gary. *Sacred Pathways: Discover Your Soul's Path to God.*

Waggoner, Brenda, and Becky Freeman. *The Velveteen Woman: Becoming Real through God's Transforming Love.*

Wright, H. Norman. *Making Peace with Your Past.*

Websites

www.keirsey.com. The Keirsey Temperament and Character website contains an online "personality sorter" to determine your type and includes information on how temperaments relate to parenting.

Two

Growth

I Want Space to Develop "Me"

*Better moms make a better world.
And a better me makes a better mom.*

MomSpeak

* My husband asked what my hobbies were and I couldn't give him an answer, other than being a mom and wife. I laid everything aside when we had our daughter.

* I'm a good mother, but I don't want to discover someday that my kids are grown and I have nothing else in my life. Working at home helps me stay in touch with an important part of myself and with the outside world.

* Before I had children I spent a lot of time doing needlework. But after my second was born, I had to force myself to finish his birth sampler. I felt that my creative side was being drowned in a sea of practicality.

* The fantasy is that your child is all you need. That your life is your child. But reality is showing me that to be a good mom, I also have to develop some other interests.

* I used to sit in the park with my baby and wonder what had happened to art, music, and politics. I felt isolated from the life I'd known for twenty years, so I decided to do something about it. One day I put my baby in the backpack and went to a show on Impressionism at the art museum.

Shannon closed the baby's door and tiptoed down the hall toward the kitchen. The muscles in the back of her neck felt tense. She raised her hand to massage them as she stood, contemplating her choices.

She had an hour. Maybe an hour and a half. After an active couple hours, Logan should sleep awhile. At thirteen months, he was into everything. Just this morning, while she was talking on the telephone, he'd committed his own version of "breaking and entering." Somehow he'd negotiated the childproof knob on the pantry, climbed up one shelf, and sprinkled a package of rice all over the pantry shelves and the kitchen floor. The cleanup had taken most of her morning.

Don't think about that now, Shannon scolded herself. *You've only got an hour, so use it.*

What she really wanted to do was to play the piano. Shannon had been a piano major in college and had taught music at the high school level for several years before she became pregnant with Logan. She was sick for most of her pregnancy, and on bed rest for the last two months, so she'd stopped teaching and even playing. Then Logan had been a hard baby, colicky and never happy unless Shannon was holding him. So that first year had felt like ten. And even now Logan was a handful. There never seemed to be time for anything but tending to him.

Today Chopin called to her from the upright in the family room. Favorite melodies played through her head, and she entered into a tug-of-war over how to spend her free moments — more frequent now that the cloud of that first year was lifting. There was a load of wash to do before the end of the day. And she really should start dinner — the process was so much easier without Logan around. After that . . . well, forget it.

Brahms beckoned her. She wavered. No. This was not the time to succumb. She needed to make out a grocery list . . . and change the kitty litter, another impossible task with Logan "helping." In fact, she really should do that first.

As she passed by the piano, however, Mozart moved her to sit down. *Well, just for a few minutes*, she rationalized. As she perched on the bench, she touched the ivory keys, then lifted her hands and played, immediately becoming lost in the music. For fifteen whole minutes, her fingers searched out the notes on the keyboard, stroking it with a rusty grace. At times, her fingers played easily. In other sections they stumbled, yet she played, building toward a loud crescendo.

She knew she should be playing like this every day! Without regular practice she couldn't expect to play well. Oh, how she longed for the freedom she once had to play and play and play.

She paused, lost in her thoughts, and then heard Logan's cries echoing down the hall. Actually, they were wails. Her playing had awakened him. And she hadn't even heard him. Now he sounded scared.

How stupid of me, she thought as she slammed the cover down over the keyboard and headed down the hall. *Now I'll never get anything done this afternoon! I shouldn't have played the piano.*

Life Lived on Hold

In this season of life, moms often pour their time into everyone and everything except themselves. The reality with babies is that their needs are many and our energy is limited.

Special needs children require even more time and energy, as do twins or triplets. And as they grow older, we still may operate as if these toddlers, young children, and our husbands can't wait for attention, but *we can.* So we may put our dreams and development on hold. Sometimes we get stuck in the distraction of the demands made upon us.

No doubt, our lives as mothers color even our language! Where once we may have carried on intellectually stimulating dialogues, we now feel that our brains are turning to mush. One writer refers to this modern affliction as "Mommy Brain." It, "like 'senior moment,' is a cheery synonym for abrupt mental decline."[1] Although we try, time is scarce for reading and keeping up on world issues, and we begin to fear we may lose the ability to think altogether! Those of us who continue to work part- or full-time after having children enjoy the connection to our life before kids, but it's never the same. We wonder whether we have enough to give the job when we're working, and enough to give the family when we're not.

We notice too the "shelving" of parts of our personhood. One mom pondered her sense that she had felt more "grown up" as a college student than she did now as a new mother. She didn't look like herself anymore, act with the confidence and intelligence she once had, or control her life as she was able to in previous years.

In finding the balance between meeting the consuming needs of young children and continuing to develop ourselves, as mothers we need the recognition and the reminder that yes, what we are doing *now* is significant. No matter how it *feels*, the time we are pouring into our children is giving them the solid, loving foundation that will buttress them for the rest of their lives. Yet we are still women, people, worthy of time and personhood. Central to our beings is the need to keep working to find the spaces within our mothering where we can tend to "me" in Mom-me.

As moms of young children, we still desire to grow and develop ourselves, both in what we do and in who we are. We have a built-in longing for self-improvement, whether that means nurturing a dream or developing more patience.

Though we enjoy investing ourselves in our families, we yearn simultaneously to reach and change and try and experiment and experience other parts of our being. To paint! To read! To think! To create! To converse! To help another! Ah ... to dream!

Season of Self-Sacrifice

Mothering, by its very nature, requires self-sacrifice. This is a season when self-fulfillment naturally conflicts with self-sacrifice. For most, this process begins with pregnancy, when the comfort and shape of the body are compromised. Emotions spin out of control. Feet swell. Abdomens distend. Blood pressure increases. And then at last, baby arrives. Along with the emotion of this miraculous event, we must make our way through weeks of soreness, bleeding, hemorrhoids, sore breasts if we nurse, and weary exhaustion.

For those who have become mothers through adoption, the sacrifice is of the heart rather than the body. Waiting for a child can be lengthy and unpredictable. And then there is the disappointment of not being part of the birth process.

Often, we make career sacrifices as well. We take time off from a job and lose touch with colleagues and developments in our field. Or we transition to work at home and must find a new rhythm in working alone, isolated from the relationships and daily camaraderie we'd known at the job. Some of us continue working outside the home, yet we too find ourselves sacrificing. It may feel like a huge sacrifice just to be away from a child during the day. Whether we've chosen to work or must do it for financial reasons, we will inevitably lose much of our own "downtime" in racing between responsibilities at home and at work. For every mom, no matter her situation, motherhood involves self-sacrifice!

Mother and author Dale Hanson Bourke warns a mother-to-be about the emotional sacrifices of mothering: "I want her to know what she will never learn in childbirth classes: that the physical wounds of childbearing will heal, but becoming a mother will leave an emotional wound so raw that she will be forever vulnerable ... that she will never read a newspaper again without asking, 'What if that had been my child?' That every plane crash, every fire will haunt her."[2]

While mothering young children, we learn plenty about giving up time and sleep. As we bathe wobbly, wrinkly babies, spoon sloppy cereal into mouths more interested in making bubbles, train resistant toddlers in the meaning of *no*, patiently watch chubby fingers master shoelaces, and then guide them as they learn to print the letters of their names—we come to know that mothering well means investing in the lives of people other than ourselves.

We know it and we do it willingly. Love is expensive. And our children are well served by mothers who are willing to give—and give *up*—freely. Yet we can't help but struggle in keeping the balance. We want to give everything to our kids, but we quickly learn the reality that we need to keep growing and becoming as well. Mothering well doesn't require us to shelve our personal needs completely. Moms too have a legitimate need to grow as individuals, to develop their talents and abilities (doing) as well as to strengthen their character (being).

Keep growing, Mom! Here are some reasons why growth can't wait until later.

You Need to Develop Yourself

Today represents an important season in your life. You can't skip it or ignore it. And you can't ignore or neglect yourself in this season, or you may find a gaping hole in the next.

You probably have dreams and desires that need to be expressed. You may have creative juices that require an outlet of expression. The "you" that has been growing since your own birth doesn't cease to exist because you've given birth to another.

Author Judith Couchman writes, "[Our family's] well-being takes priority over most pursuits, and I believe God honors decisions that place people above accomplishments. On the other hand, it also takes balance not to worship at the shrine of family to the exclusion of other relationships and responsibilities. It is possible to isolate ourselves within the family structure, hiding from personal growth and spiritual calling."[3]

Another writer, Katrina Kenison, encourages balance as well, asking, "What are the things you most love to do? Are you doing them? If not, make at least one of them a top priority. Balance means taking care of yourself as well as those who are dependent on you for their well-being."[4]

What Every **MOM** Needs

If you wonder whether you have the energy or the mental or emotional capacity it will take to grow personally in the midst of your mothering, think again. Journalist Katherine Ellison has written an entire book on the amazing new research that finds women who become mothers experience a reshaping of the brain in which it becomes a more complex organ — mothers actually get smarter rather than dumber or more spacey! "By means of a dynamic combination of love, genes, hormones, and practice, the female brain undergoes concrete and likely long-lasting changes through the process of giving birth and raising children," she writes.[5] You *do* have what it takes to grow, Mom, and you will be the first to benefit from your own growth!

Your Family Needs You to Develop Yourself

Every member of your family will benefit from the "you" that you are becoming! Your family will also benefit from the wholeness of your example. They need the challenge and inspiration of your growth in order to grow themselves.

While at times it might seem that investing in yourself is an abandonment of others in your life, the truth is that when you invest in your own growth, you are more able to influence the growth of those around you. They learn to take care of themselves as they see you balancing the need to care for others as well as for yourself.

Author Deena Lee Wilson urges mothers, in the spirit of Virginia Woolf, to keep "a room of your own" to be and to grow and to develop. "I know that each time I send myself to my room, little eyes are watching me and drawing big conclusions. Maybe Chandler and Ethan can just grow up knowing the truth that ease is a holy art to be learned and that quiet time and play, naps and wonder are for big people, too. I hope it becomes as natural as breathing to them to care for and water the gardens of their own souls."[6]

Your World Needs You to Develop Yourself

All around you are those who need what you have to offer. Whether it's a finely tuned skill or just a natural outgrowth of the person you are, your contribution to the lives of others is increased when you develop yourself. Whether you receive a paycheck for your contribution or simply a "thank you" now and then, what you possess is what you need to invest in the world around you. "A woman who keeps a sensible piece of herself to herself finds peace to give away to her world."[7]

Seeing you interact with confidence, using innate gifts and learned skills, will encourage others to discover ways in which they can improve their own lives and relationships. You may not think it is worth much, but to someone who is watching, your example is valuable.

God Desires Our Growth

Above all, it is God's plan for us to grow. "God loves us where we are, but he loves us too much to leave us there," reads a popular wall hanging. The goal of the Christian life is to become more and more like Jesus, possessing character qualities that he possessed like love, joy, peace, patience, kindness, and goodness. The mothering season of life offers fertile soil for all of these. And Drs. Henry Cloud and John Townsend, in their book *How People Grow*, remind us, "God is the source of life. He is the source of growth as well."[8] Yet growth doesn't come without a struggle.

Growing Pains

As exciting and fulfilling as developing our potential might be, it is also painful. Growing hurts. It stretches us in new directions. It uses muscles, both mental and emotional, which may have atrophied from lack of use. It demands risks that may leave us feeling vulnerable and exposed. As one mom lamented, "I often wonder whether I have done the right thing when faced with so many choices."

Change is often both inconvenient and uncomfortable. We may have grown in many ways before becoming mothers only to find out that vast new areas of growth remain. Keeping a busy household organized and running. Making new mom friends outside of a school or workplace setting. Finding and using a method of child discipline that is healthier than the one your parents used. Making money stretch farther than you've ever had to before. Finding a way to finish a degree or begin a home business while cherishing this season with young children. Caring for aging parents while focusing on children full of needs. Keeping that spark of personal passion and giftedness alive. Clearly, our need for growth is never ending, yet the means of gaining that growth and measuring it may seem murkier than ever.

Realizations like these may be difficult.

Growth Is Slow

It takes time to grow. In the stage of life when our young children are growing like weeds, personal growth can seem like a bonsai tree.

Authors John and Stasi Eldredge encourage, "The world needs your beauty. That is why you are here. Your heart and your beauty are something to be treasured and nourished. And it takes time. Every gardener knows this. In our age of instant makeovers and microwave meals, we don't like to wait. But a newly planted rose's presentation in its first year is nothing compared to its second. If properly cared for, its second year's display doesn't hold a candle to its third. Gardens need to become established; their roots need to go deep through summer rains and winter frosts. A garden's beauty does not diminish with age; rather it takes years for it to become all that it can become."[9] And so it is for us, mothers. In the busyness of growing our children, the seeds of our own growth can take root and sprout given the care of time and persistence.

Growth Is Hard to Measure

There are many hectic days when you can hardly tell if you're growing or shrinking. You can stand your three-year-old against the wall and see tangible evidence of his growth by marking a spot two inches above the measurement made last year. But you look at your own life, and all you can see growing is the hair on your legs!

The intangibility of the growth of character makes sticking with our goals seem discouraging. Infants don't praise us when we master patience or excellence in child care. And when we go to the wall to mark our progress, the results of our efforts may not even be noticeable.

Growth Is Costly

Whether developing dreams or character, growth will cost us something. If you're earning credit toward a college degree, squeezing in a part-time job (or juggling a full-time career), or partnering with a friend to do some volunteer work, you can

What Every **MOM** Needs

expect to make some tough choices. Like the choice to read a book during your child's naptime and then to buy take-and-bake pizza instead of making a meal. Or if you're learning to set healthy boundaries in relationships, you'll have to risk losing a friendship or unsettling a family relationship. If you're recovering from a childhood where a parent had an addiction, you may be moving away from a tendency toward codependent behavior and will have to expend personal energy and experience discomfort in forming new ways of relating with others. Maybe you've realized that an area of anger in your life is hurting you more than the one you're angry at, and you're learning to forgive. It will cost you some pride and a commitment to letting go of feelings that may keep coming back. Growth always costs us something, but then, there is almost always a cost to what is of value.

Along with making costly choices comes the reality of accepting the consequences for such choices. Your husband may be disappointed with "pizza again" (though the kids probably won't be!). Or you may really lose that friend. Or a family member may begin giving you the cold shoulder.

In his book *The Pursuit of Excellence*, Ted Engstrom writes, "Every truly worthwhile achievement of excellence has a price tag. The question you must answer for yourself is, How much am I willing to pay in hard work, patience, sacrifice and endurance to be a person of excellence?"[10]

Slow, hard to measure, costly—growth often brings pain along with its rewards.

Dreaming Dreams

So? Dreams make the difference between living a life and really *living* a life. But some of us, caught up in the busyness of childrearing, have forgotten how to dream. Here are some suggestions:

Dare to Dream

Identify where you want to grow and then start dreaming about possibilities for getting there. One writer comments, "We must dream, because we are made in the image of him who sees things that are not and wills them to be."[11]

Find a quiet spot. Sit back and let your thoughts roam. What has God already done in your life? What might he still do? Consider, just for a moment, what isn't but could be. Dream beyond where you are. You stand before your children as probably the most influential person of their lifetime. You are leading the way in teaching them what it means to be an adult, to be a living, learning, ever-changing, and growing individual. So what are you doing to influence them to be lifelong learners and seekers and explorers?

Dreams begin with asking such questions as, "If you could do anything you wanted with an extra hour today, what would it be?" Sometimes dreams have their roots in the past. "When you think back over your childhood, what did you do with your spare time?" Dreams also peer around the corners of our lives and right into the places where we live for clues as to how we can grow. As one mom says, "I need to hold on to *my* passions and interests and actually seek those out."

If you have trouble identifying the growth spots in your life, check the Mom Me Time section at the end of this chapter. As Barbara Sher encourages in her book *Wishcraft*, the important thing is to find what you love. "There may be several things ... whatever they are—guitar music, bridges, bird-watching, sewing, the stock market, the history of India—there is a very, very good reason why you love them. Each one is a clue to something inside you: a talent, an ability, a way of seeing the world that is uniquely yours."[12]

Identify where you want to grow. Then start dreaming a dream for your life and make a plan. Judith Couchman stresses that God "designed us to be purposeful, granting us the capacity to grow socially, emotionally, spiritually, and intellectually throughout our lives. Jesus never taught us to be comfortable and maintain the status quo. He commanded us to go, grow, and change the world. Inertia is our choice."[13]

Sequence Your Dreams

Once you've settled on an area of potential growth, break it down into small sections. We all know that the years of mothering young children are packed full with responsibilities and urgent tasks. If we set out to accomplish gargantuan achievements during these years, we'll probably be disappointed, because something will suffer—our children, our marriages, our dreams, or our health.

Let's not forget that although one or more areas of our own growth may slow down or be put on hold, many other areas of our growth as moms and women will be moving at full speed. Parenting grows us in more ways than perhaps any other undertaking of our lives!

Socially, we've allowed brand new, important little persons into our lives and we need to get to know them. Spiritually and emotionally we have new and intense challenges in the areas of patience and perseverance. We're growing in all that it means to be a parent and to discipline and nurture and teach. We're learning how our individual personalities and strengths uniquely fit us for a particular style of parenting. And we're learning how to grow and compensate in those areas where we're weak. We're learning how to manage a household, with all the multitasking and various skills required. And we're learning how to live and move in the world outside our homes in ways that are realistic and beneficial for our growing family.

You've probably heard analogies about life being like a book, with each stage of development occupying its own chapter. During your early life, you eagerly scribbled out your contribution on the clean pages of the first few chapters. But with the arrival of children, your own journaling changes its focus some, and also offers the time and space for you to help your child hold his crayon, poised and eager to write in his book of days.

Rather than setting your own journal completely aside for these next few years of child rearing, why not carefully slot time to record a few paragraphs — perhaps a single page or even a whole chapter? We can make progress toward our dreams a little at a time.

This idea of outlining life in chapters — breaking it down into sections — is sometimes called sequencing. This means giving priority to children when they are young. Then, as they grow up, we have more time for other pursuits, including the development of our dreams.

Tell Someone Else about Your Dreams

Everyone needs someone to champion their dreams, someone to encourage them to keep dreaming when they're not sure they can. One mother describes the importance of having such friends when her circumstances forced her to give up a dream: "Music had always been in my life. I played several instruments in various groups. In my late twenties I developed MS, which made it impossible to play and perform. Through the encouragement of friends, I discovered I have other talents, especially singing."

Dottie McDowell, wife of Josh McDowell, describes how her mother always valued what Dottie valued: "As an adult, she still dreams my dreams, wanting to know every detail and delighting in every interest that I pursue. Does this communicate that my dreams and goals have significance? You bet it does! Has that had a positive impact on my self-image — even as an adult? Of course."[14]

Maybe you have a good friend who is also dreaming while mothering. Maybe your husband knows the gifts within you and longs with you for them to be developed. Maybe your mother or aunt or sister remembers your dream and will remind you of your personal potential. Seek someone in your life who can help to keep your dream alive.

Get Growing!

We were created by God to grow and change and develop. We all have great, untapped potential. As William James once observed, "Compared with what we ought to be, we are only half awake. Our fires are damped, our drafts are checked. We are making use of only a small part of our possible mental and physical resources."

So spend some Mom Me Time, and nurture your need to grow.

Mom Me Time

Mom Me Time 1
Barriers to Growth

Sometimes we are the ones getting in the way of our growth. Do you possess personal attitudes or behaviors that are keeping you from growing? Author Judith Couchman suggests several barriers to growth. Do any of these barriers threaten your growth? Check those that may apply to you. Then think about how you can eliminate this barrier. Talk with a friend or your husband about the hold this barrier has on your personal growth.

❑ Busyness
❑ Competitiveness
❑ Disbelief
❑ Emotional wounds
❑ Fear of failure
❑ Fear of success
❑ Health limitations
❑ Jealousy
❑ Lack of discipline

❑ Lack of finances
❑ Laziness
❑ Low self-esteem
❑ People's opinions
❑ Resentment
❑ Self-pity
❑ Pride
❑ Worry
❑ Wrong location[15]

Mom Me Time 2
Keep Dreaming!

Are you still dreaming? Maybe you need to uncover some new dreams. Consider these questions and ideas to help you identify an area of passion and potential in your life:

What Every **MOM** Needs

1. Is there a subject that always sparked your interest? What is it?

2. What did you daydream about as a child?

3. List ten positive personal characteristics. Do these traits suggest any talents or skills worth pursuing? Ask a friend to add to the list.

4. Write down twenty-five things you want to do before you die. Narrow the list to ten, then five. Then rank in order of importance.[16]

Mom Me Time 3
Find a Growin' Girlfriend

Think for a moment about the people in your life. Who else is interested in growing? Who might have a dream yet to be realized? Jot down a name or two here.

Make a phone call or send an e-mail and ask this friend if she would be your designated "growin' girlfriend." Make a plan to meet at Starbucks once a month, or e-mail monthly updates and encourage one another in taking even small steps toward your dream or the growth you desire.

Mom Me Time 4
Develop Critical Thinking Skills

An important part of growing in life involves decision making. Mothers make decisions every day. Here are some suggestions for evaluating choices and making wise decisions.

1. Pinpoint the problem. State specifically what it is you need to decide.
2. Set a deadline. Give yourself a "due date" for your decision. Develop a timeline.
3. Gather information. What are your sources? Where can you get the facts?
4. List the pros and cons. What are the positive and negative aspects of each alternative?
5. Ask tough questions. Evaluate your options according to your values. Does this fit? Is it wise? Does it conflict with biblical truth?
6. Make a decision. Move forward in a direction with confidence that you've done the best job you can.

What Every **MOM** Needs

Mom Me Time 5
Find a Mentor

Determine your mentoring needs. Do you need a coach, an encourager, a counselor, or someone to listen to your ideas? Do you want to sharpen your leadership or parenting skills, gifts, or spiritual depth? Your needs and goals will determine what kind of mentor is best. You don't need a mentor unless you have goals.

Who are the resourceful people you already know and respect? An aunt or close relative? A godly woman? An older neighbor or friend? Relationships and resourcefulness act as magnets and serve as the basis of the mentoring relationship. Look for women six to fifteen years older than you are. Too much older, and she will be part of an unfamiliar generation. Too much younger, and she will be too much like a peer. Sometimes you can be mentored by a woman younger than yourself if she has unusual qualities or expertise.

Look for women who are living your dream or share in your dream. Share your desires and objectives with potential mentors. Many older women will be flattered that you consider them worthy of your consideration. Remember, they have a need for generativity—impacting the succeeding generation.

Be willing to pay the price to be mentored. This includes flexibility and commitment. If she jogs, jog with her. Offer to work on a project together so you can help her as you learn from her. Approach your time together with specific needs and questions. A resourceful person will be able to give you great input without formal preparation. Your initiative and intentionality will speed and enhance the mentoring process.[17]

Mom Me Time 6
Make It Visual

Do you have photos, clippings, or other trinkets that remind you of where you want to grow or what you've begun to dream? Purchase a small French memo board and begin slipping these visual reminders into the board. Use it as a visual reminder to keep moving toward your dream. Remember God's promise: "He who began a good work in you will carry it on to completion until the day of Christ Jesus" (Philippians 1:6).

HOLD FAST YOUR DREAM
by Louise Driscoll

Hold fast your dream!
Within your heart
Keep one still secret spot
Where dreams may go,
And sheltered so,
May thrive and grow —
Where doubt and fear are not.
Oh, keep a place apart
Within your heart,
For little dreams to go.[18]

Mom We Time

Dim the lights and light a few candles. In the quiet, reach back together to that time in your life B.C. — Before Children. What were your dreams? Did you have a plan for what you would be doing at age twenty-five, thirty, forty? Light a candle you can pass around, and as each one holds the candle, tell the others about your earlier dreams. Are these dreams still burning strong? Have they changed? Are they just barely smoldering embers left in the dust of a much earlier phase of your journey?

Stand back from your life for a moment. Glance back at the section on why your growth can't wait, pages 62–64. As you peer into your life from the outside, would you say that the greatest reason your own personal growth can't wait is for the sake of:

* You?
* Your family?
* Your world?
* God?

Tell the others about why you answered the way you did.

As you consider your own growth, what is most frustrating at this stage of your life? Is it the slow rate of growth you seem destined to accept? Is it your inability to measure any growth you do achieve? Is it the high cost of attempting to grow?

Talk together about the challenges you encounter when it comes to growing "you." Encourage each other not to lose sight of your dreams!

For Further Reading

Books

Bolles, Richard. *What Color Is Your Parachute? A Practical Manual for Job-Hunters and Career-Changers.*

Chambers, Oswald. *My Utmost for His Highest.*

Cloud, Henry, and John Townsend. *How People Grow: What the Bible Reveals about Personal Growth.*

Couchman, Judith. *Designing a Woman's Life: Discovering Your Unique Purpose and Passion.*

Eldridge, John. *Journey of Desire: Searching for the Life We Only Dreamed Of.*

——. *Waking the Dead: The Glory of a Heart Fully Alive.*

Ellison, Katherine. *The Mommy Brain: How Motherhood Makes Us Smarter.*

Morgan, Elisa. *Naked Fruit: Getting Honest about the Fruit of the Spirit.*

Parrott, Les, III. *Coulda, Shoulda, Woulda: Live in the Present, Find Your Future.*

Sher, Barbara, with Annie Gottlieb. *Wishcraft: How to Get What You Really Want.*

Warren, Rick. *The Purpose Driven Life: What on Earth Am I Here For?*

Websites

www.christiancourses.com. Offers free online courses to grow in personal skills (such as public speaking) and also in biblical knowledge and other Christian topics.

www.relevantmagazine.com. This website has a section on "Life" that offers personal growth articles on relationships, health, career, and finance from a contemporary Christian perspective.

Three

Relationship

I Want Someone to Understand Me

*No mom is an island. Without people in my life
who know me and love me, I can't be me.*

MomSpeak

* Keeping up with the kids isn't the hardest part of mothering; it's the loneliness.
* Most of my friends work, so there's no time for friendship, except at night when I'm too tired.
* I need a good support system of other moms with babies who aren't afraid to talk about the personal issues we all share.
* After moving to our fourth home in four years with children ages one and four, the thought of making new friends was too overwhelming. So I just stayed at home with the kids and felt lonely.
* My husband says he feels like I love our children more than him, and fear grips my heart when I realize that he might be right.
* Even when my baby is asleep, I have no time for my husband because one ear is always tuned to listen for her cry. I find myself worthless as a sexual partner because I can't stop thinking about the baby.
* I have many friends and I cherish each one. But I pray to meet a friend who can be my best friend. Her husband and my husband click, our children get along. We spend time together shopping, having coffee, laughing ...

Five-thirty. Dinnertime. Well, at least she'd made it this far. Corinne opened the refrigerator and surveyed the boring contents. *It's so hard to cook for just me and the kids*, she thought. *I hate it when Jack is out of town.* But then, it was more than dinnertime that made Corinne miss Jack.

Making a quick decision, she called to Jackson and Jenna, "Hey, kids! We're going to McDonald's!" Whoops and hollers preceded their wild dash for the car. Corinne gathered up little Jillian in her infant seat, grabbed her purse, and followed. *I guess we'll all survive a night of fast food*, she reasoned as she flipped off the lights and pulled the door shut, hoping to leave her loneliness behind.

The parking lot was crowded, so she cautioned Jackson and Jenna to hold hands and walk in front of her. In line, Corinne held the infant seat and gently guided the other two until they reached the front, where she ordered Happy Meals and a salad.

They all slid into a booth, and Corinne placed Jillian, still strapped into her seat, next to her. Then Corinne began the task of squeezing out catsup, securing crooked lids on drinks, and pushing napkins at greasy fingers.

Jackson and Jenna ate a few bites of their burgers and fries while playing with their meal toys, and then begged to go to the play area. Since she could keep an eye on them through the window near the booth, Corinne agreed.

Glancing around the crowded room, she saw—in the booth diagonal to hers—a young mom and dad holding hands while smiling at their chubby-faced toddler. One table down was a group of loud teenagers, cocky and oblivious to all around them. Behind her, another mom appeared to be in deep conversation with her preteen daughter. Everyone she saw seemed content and connected to someone.

Corinne felt a familiar longing. Loneliness. It seemed absurd. How could she sit in this room filled with people and feel alone? How could she *ever* feel lonely with three children around every minute?

She looked toward the play area. Jackson and Jenna were playing happily. Jillian had dozed off in her infant seat. Corinne sighed and idly played with her straw. *Why didn't I bring a book?* With her index finger, she plugged the top of the straw, then lifted it from her Diet Coke and let the liquid trickle out. People came and went through the restaurant doors. Meanwhile, her loneliness lingered.

Stop! Corinne scolded herself. *You have three healthy kids, a husband with a good job. Isn't that enough?* It should be, she reasoned, yet she longed for someone to talk to. Someone who would understand her fears and her struggles with contentment and patience.

Just then, a woman about her age, carrying a tray laden with two Happy Meals and a salad, slid into the booth next to hers. Two little boys—about five and seven years old—followed. From the mother's face, Corinne could tell she was a woman who loved what she was doing, even as she patiently squeezed out catsup, straightened crooked lids on drinks, and pushed napkins at greasy fingers.

When her boys ran off to the play area, the woman looked up and her eyes met Corinne's. Across the cluttered table, she smiled. "So you're eating gourmet tonight too?"

Corinne laughed and suddenly felt better. Here they were—total strangers. They would probably never see each other again. But in those few words, Corinne felt understood for the first time in ages.

That One and Only Lonely Feeling

Mothers of preschoolers overwhelmingly report that one of their greatest struggles is with loneliness, a feeling of being disconnected or isolated. Though the words may vary, the feelings describe a common need for relationship—the desire to share life with others and be understood.

Marla Paul, a newspaper columnist, tells the story of her loneliness after relocating to a new city with her husband and young daughter. When, after many attempts, she couldn't seem to forge friendships with other moms around her, she wrote about her "wallflower status" in an essay for the city newspaper. Within days she was flooded with phone calls, letters, and testimonies in person about similar feelings and experiences. "I'd yanked the curtain off a shameful secret, only there is nothing shameful about it. A lot of women are lonely. And it's ... hard to make friends in our culture of busyness. As we frantically juggle a constellation of demands many of us are unwilling, or unable, to fold a new pal into our lives."[1]

When we're lonely it feels like a key ingredient for living has been sucked from our lives, leaving us exposed and unprotected. That feeling of being alone is awful because we're not getting what we intrinsically need as humans. God made us for relationship. "Either we can live as unique members of a connected community, experiencing the fruit of Christ's life within us, or we can live as terrified, demanding, self-absorbed islands, disconnected from community and desperately determined to get by with whatever resources we brought to our island with us," says psychologist Larry Crabb. "The longing to connect defines our dignity as human beings and our destiny as image bearers [of God]."[2]

In other words, our need for connection is a need created within us by God. And this need or *longing* is answered by a sense of *belonging,* which is also known as being in community. We are said to be in community when we are connected to others in some context of meaningful relationships in which we have a sense of belonging and a shared sense of nurturing and being nurtured.

For most of us women today, relationships are just about as important as the air we breathe. So it hits us hard when we become moms and find that the circumstances of child rearing, the pace, and the energy required throw some serious challenges at our relational connections. We find our friendships, our relationships with extended family, and our marriages challenged by all that is required of us as mothers.

Yet we can't give up on being in relationship and even nurturing our relationships. Doing so would be the death of a big part of ourselves! Let's take a look at why this is true.

Relationship in All Its Many Colors

It used to be that, before marriage and children, when women thought about the word *relationship*, it probably meant a coveted connection with a guy. We longed for a relationship with the opposite sex to fill that particular relational desire. And we longed for a lot more—like marriage. Relationship with a man involved physical intimacy—sex in all its fulfillment. And still today, this kind of relationship is an important part of who we are as women in relationship. But the man in our life will never be all we need.

Today, as grown women and mothers, we may also think of our friendships with our mothers, our sisters, our neighbors, and our girlfriends when we consider the importance of relationship in our lives. And if we're honest and look carefully, we see that we need more than just a husband or a mother or a best friend to engage the various parts of ourselves. We need many and varied people who know and can connect with the parts of us that make us who we are, a variety of people who can love us as we continue to grow and change.

As one mom said, "After I had my first baby I felt that my whole outlook was changing. I was suddenly needed for everything my little baby did. One day everything was going wrong. My son wouldn't have anything to do with me—I—the one who did everything for him. I couldn't get him to eat, to stop crying. If I tried to hold him, he screamed and kicked at me. I called my mother, crying uncontrollably, and asked her to please come over and help me, to tell me what I was doing wrong. She managed to calm my son and me, then she just listened and nodded every now and then to everything I felt and said."

We can't make it without those moms or friends or husbands who will simply "be" with us as we travel this road of motherhood with its tiring, confusing, exasperating, and also wonderful and unforgettable twists and turns.

Stumbling Blocks to Relationships

Even as we recognize our need for relationship, we find some obstacles that block our pathway to experiencing relationship with others.

✳ *I'm too tired to be friendly.* There's no arguing with the reality that moms of preschoolers have very little energy to spend on building and maintaining friendships, and even extended family relationships and marriages. After four nights with little sleep because of a teething, fussy six-month-old, keeping up with the constant responsibility of putting meals on the table, cleaning up, and doing laundry, we feel we have little energy left over for pouring into relationships. Writer Laura Jensen Walker expresses her experience when a close friend became a mother. "It was like she'd dropped off the face of the earth. Katie was completely incommunicado for the first six or seven weeks of little Jacqueline's life."[3]

Certainly that feeling of being "incommunicado" can last well past six or seven weeks. And it's not only our friends who lose out. As moms we're often too tired even to relate well to our husbands. One mom recalls, "With the onset of parenthood, I often felt tired and put my husband in last place. I remember one particularly exhausting day when by the time we got into bed, all I wanted to do was sleep. That's not what he had in mind, but I was too tired to care."

✳ *I don't want to risk making a friend because one of us will just move away.* In our mobile society, we may not stay in one place long enough to put down the roots necessary to build relationships. We may be separated from our hometowns and the long-term relationships with people who "knew us when," and we fear that we can never be "known" again. Even moves within the same city and transitions from working to staying at home, or vice versa, can make it difficult to maintain ongoing friendships. And starting over can feel more difficult each time.

"We moved to a new city about a year ago, and I remember looking out the window and seeing a woman jogging with her child," one mom recalls. "I thought seriously about tackling her and making her talk to me ... yet I never did try to meet her."

✳ *I don't have time to be friendly.* Marla Paul, author of *The Friendship Crisis*, observes, "Employed, married women with children are the most free-time-deprived people in the country."[4] If we're employed and mothering, we let go of friendships in order to survive.

On the other hand, if we're mothering without external employment, we often look around the neighborhood, only to find that no one else is available during the few precious daytime moments we could be free. And when a husband comes home, his needs and the needs of the children come first, ahead of time and attention to friends.

Often, those of us who have been close to our mothers or sisters find that it's even hard to spend the time on the phone or in person that we had enjoyed in the past. The kids fight or whine while we try and talk on the phone, and we decide it's not worth the effort. Trying to work visits around daytime naps, preschool schedules, and early bedtimes can make seeing family feel impossible.

✳ *It's too much trouble—or disappointing—to be friendly.* Some of us defeat ourselves, not embracing the very thing we need because it's too much trouble—or too disappointing. A newspaper article about loneliness explains: "Lonely people are more critical of themselves, more disappointed with others and less willing to take risks in social situations. They are afraid of closeness and actually talk themselves out of being connected to others. They'd rather feel depressed and alone than risk rejection."5

Sometimes we idealize a friend, but then that friend lets us down and we decide not to go deeper in friendship because it's too much trouble to patch it up or accept our differences. And then, women can be so competitive, especially moms who assume *their* way of mothering is the only right way. Sometimes it's easier not to engage with them than to put up with their need to be right.

Licensed counselor Sharon Hersh, in her book *Bravehearts: Unlocking the Courage to Love with Abandon*, explains that women who have a high need for control often pull out of relationships because they are risky and can't be controlled. They then acquire an attitude of independence. "When independence becomes the life force of the heart, the result is a determination never to be vulnerable, needy, or burdensome. The energy of the heart is expended to keep people at a distance and often looks for an excuse to be more focused on tasks than on relationships."6 Certainly, as moms of young children we can relate to the feelings of being vulnerable and needy. But in not wanting to be real about our struggles, we often cut off the very people in our lives who are feeling the same way!

✳ *My children are my best friends.* Some moms admit that in this season, their children are their best buddies. After all, we spend more time with them than anyone else, so can't we find some of our relational fulfillment there? No! Can we enjoy our kids and find fulfillment in parenting? Sure. Time spent with our kids will bring many enjoyable moments, and our roles as mothers should bring a certain level of fulfillment. But our children are not given to us to meet our relational

What Every **MOM** Needs

needs. They should not feel that kind of pressure. "Children do not exist to please us," writes author and professor Walter Wangerin. "They are not for us at all, but rather we exist for them, to protect them now and prepare them for the future."[7] We'll be better moms when our connections with adults are meeting our relational needs.

We're too tired, we live in a transient society, we don't have time, we're uncomfortable—for a number of obvious reasons, we struggle with relationship. Yet our desire won't go away. As Sharon Hersh writes about the many hours she has spent with women clients, "I have discovered that deep within every woman is a heart full of longing for relationships."[8]

Making Relationship Happen

So how can we be sure our longings for relationship are met? Let's accept that our relationships now may look different than relationships we've had in the past. A close friendship may develop on the front sidewalk with a neighbor, day after sunny day as we help our children learn to ride their tricycles. We may go deeper with a longtime, long-distance friend only through e-mails written when kids are in bed and we finally have some quiet moments. And a marriage that once enjoyed long leisurely hours of one-on-one time may keep its relational spark through short phone calls squeezed into busy days and occasional evenings and weekends away squeezed into full calendars.

Although the time and space for relationships may feel less than ideal, we can find ways to keep relating and growing together. We can keep working at relationships that are deeper and more satisfying.

Friendships

We couldn't live without our girlfriends! This need for close female relationship started early in life. Most of us remember our "first best friend" from preadolescence, a friend with whom we shared secrets, wrote notes, and had weekend sleepovers. During the teenage years, our best friends started competing with boyfriends, a competition that often lasted through our dating years and the first few years of marriage. But now another stage has begun. As moms and women, we can identify with each other in ways our husbands just can't. We really need close women friends again because we want to feel understood.

Once we understand the possible barriers to healthy friendship, where do we start in making close friends for this stage of our journey?

❋ *If you want a friend, be a friend.* Figure out what you value most in a friendship and then work on developing and modeling those qualities yourself. Remember that many other women out there are in need of a friend too. Move your focus from yourself and your needs to others and their needs. Do for someone else what you would appreciate someone doing for you. In the process, you will find you have planted the seed for some budding friendships.

❋ *Seek friends on "common ground."* During this season of life, moms need other moms to share their joys and struggles. Seek friends with common circumstances, such as other moms who have just given birth to a first child or other moms with "special needs" children. Look for mothers' groups that meet your unique needs. For example, MOPS is an organization designed for mothers of preschoolers. MOPS groups meet in churches, homes, and workplaces all around the country. Call a local church or the international headquarters of MOPS (303-733-5353), or go online to www.MOPS.org and find out about groups that meet in your area.

✵ *Hold friends loosely.* Sometimes we tend to get possessive with our friends. This response may come from the desire for a single "best friend" and expectation that another will be a best and *only* friend. In friendship, possessiveness suffocates. The mark of the most mature friendship may be the open-handedness of sharing our friends with other friends, with the knowledge that different friends with different personalities meet our different needs.

✵ *Some friends are seasonal.* Some friends move away. Life situations change. One woman might have been an intimate friend in the workplace, but now that you're a mom, temporarily at home, you may have less in common. Or one mom might have been a friend while your children were in preschool together, but now you've gone your separate ways, and you have less in common. One woman recently differentiated between "friends for the road" and "friends for the heart." Not every friend is meant to be our best friend, and not every friendship is meant to be forever. Writer Elizabeth Cody Newenhuyse notes, " 'Friends for the road' are the people God puts in our life for a short time or a specific purpose. But a friend for the heart ... that's the friendship that's meant to last."[9]

✵ *Open yourself to unexpected friendships.* If a person of another culture, another faith, another generation, or another background lands in your life, you'll have an opportunity to make an unexpected friendship. Sure, there may be some challenges. You'll have to stretch beyond your world and maybe adjust your perspective some, but these special friendships can enlarge and encourage us as well.

Marriage

Here's one of the most obvious "duh" statements of this book: Children change our marriages! They change who we are; they change our priorities and all of our relationships. Sometimes in the midst of these changes, we find ourselves counting on our girlfriends more than our husbands for understanding. But when we transfer a relationship of emotional intimacy from a husband to a friend, we border on the problem of committing *emotional* adultery. For the married woman, friendships are meant to complement and complete the need for relational intimacy, not replace it altogether so that emotional intimacy is unnecessary or neglected in the marriage relationship.

One woman admitted that her friends "husbanded" her through the early years of her marriage when her husband was a medical intern and largely unavailable to her. While this kind of help is comforting and meets an immediate need, it may also rob a woman of establishing that kind of intimacy with her husband.

Our bond with our life partner is the most important source of relationship. Yet a satisfying relationship in marriage is often a struggle. Why? Part of the answer may exist in our culture or personal history.

The astounding divorce rate in our society makes marriage feel like a less-than-safe place. For many of us moms, our first experience of marriage—the marriage of our parents—was not so positive. Many of us come from divorced homes, and we feel sometimes that building a different marriage and a different life for our children is a strenuous walk through uncharted territory.

Then there's the fact that men and women often interpret quality relationships differently. When one partner seeks intimate relationship, he may be looking for companionship or sex. For the other, intimacy may mean the close connection of being understood.

Lorilee Craker writes, "Girls, we know if we've just had a fight, big or small, and the making up hasn't been adequate, we ain't doing the deed with him no matter how long it's been! Women usually need to feel emotionally close to their lovers to want sex. We simply must be on the same page, feeling like partners in regard to the house and the kids, for us to give of ourselves in a sexual way. A husband will typically operate in reverse manner. Our men need to feel close to us physically before they invest a great deal of emotional energy in their marriages."[10]

How Children Change a Marriage

Children change the marriage relationship in some wonderful ways. As author Dale Hanson Bourke tells a friend contemplating motherhood: "My friend's relationship with her husband will change, but not in the ways she thinks. I wish she could understand how much more you can love a man who is always careful to powder the baby or who never hesitates to play with his son or daughter. I think she should know that she will fall in love with her husband again for reasons she would now find very unromantic."[11]

There's another response, however. The "down" side of the up-and-downness of adjusting to a new baby brings all those stumbling blocks to intimacy we've already discussed, such as fatigue, lack of time, changes in priorities, and perceived lack of understanding. Slowly a husband and wife may realize that their communication patterns have changed. They are less intimate, more custodial. As one woman shared:

> My husband and I have such mechanical con-
> versations these days, mostly about our kids and our
> responsibilities. "Did you mail that package? We need
> more dog food. What shall we do about Allison's tan-
> trums?" The other day I asked him what he wanted
> for his birthday.
>
> "I don't know," he answered.
>
> "Please tell me something," I begged, "because I'm
> going out tomorrow afternoon and I have to get you
> something."
>
> "Don't bother," he said. "It's gotten too mechani-
> cal ... just like everything else around here."
>
> And I felt really hurt.

Drs. Les and Leslie Parrott, codirectors of the Center for Relationship Development at Seattle Pacific University, explain, "Studies show that when baby makes three, conflicts increase eightfold: marriage takes a backseat; women feel over-burdened and men feel shoved aside. By the baby's first birth-day, most mothers are less happy about their marriage, and some are wondering whether their marriage will even make it. Baby-induced marital meltdowns are not uncommon."[12]

Another mom puts words to the Parrotts' findings. "John and I have enjoyed marriage and struggled to understand what other married couples argue about vehemently. Needless to say, our honeymoon was an extended one. The day our baby arrived, we suddenly seemed to find an accumulation of differences we had no idea existed. We have to keep reminding ourselves that we are on the same team; we're in this together."

Many moms admit falling in love with their new babies, the kind of surprising, consuming love that sometimes closed out their husbands. "Is anything easier than sliding into a pattern of putting our kids before their dad?" asks Lorilee Craker. "It's so simple that a surprising number of moms do so without even realizing it. A child needs to be fed, changed, dressed, rocked.... His needs are never-ending, and he's so helpless. After all, your guy is a grown man, totally capable of taking care of himself. But the little ones need Mom to do just about everything for them. Or do they? Kids require that we meet their basic needs of being fed, clothed, loved, and set on the right path, but one of the main things they need is for Mom and Dad to love each other and build a strong relationship with each other. This they need infinitely more than they need your being home every night of the week catering to their every whim."[13]

Is There Sex after Kids?

In our book *Real Moms*, we entitled one chapter "Viagra Mom," and we talk about the reality that sex changes when children come into a marriage. Especially when children are very young, we often don't have the sexual appetite that we may have had previously. We're tired. We're distracted. Our bodies feel used up by our children long before bedtime, and the last thing we may feel like doing many nights is "giving out" some more in a physical way.

But someone else in the marriage may feel completely differently. Our husbands often experience less physical and mental exhaustion from children than we do. Their testosterone levels remain the same, and their biggest frustration is that they're having to share their wife's time. They may feel they're not even getting equal time.

"My body was in constant use by the baby," said one mom. "So when my husband came on to me, it felt like one more person needing something from me. I was touched out by the end of the day."

Our hormones often contribute to our lack of desire as well. A woman's estrogen level, the lifeline for sexual desire, plummets after she gives birth and only begins to increase again as the ovaries resume their function. This can take from a month to a year after childbirth, depending on whether she breastfeeds or not. For those who do nurse, a hormone called prolactin has been found to greatly lower libido as well, while also decreasing the production of the body's natural lubricants.[14]

If sex has never been pleasurable for you, this area of your marriage may need some outside help. A small group of women do experience continuing pain with sex long after childbirth, and some have found that even their gynecologists don't understand this pain. A condition called vaginismus may be the reason, and can be helped with physical treatment and possibly counseling.[15] If you and your husband have always been on

What Every **MOM** Needs

different pages regarding sex and you don't see that changing, it may get worse with the addition of children to your marriage. Sweeping these issues under the rug won't get rid of them. Rather, they will likely mushroom over time and may put your marriage into crisis down the road. Check out the reading list at the end of this chapter. Confide in a wise friend. Talk with a trusted leader in your church. Consider meeting with a professional marriage and family counselor. Your marriage can grow healthy and strong when you give it the attention it needs.

Steps toward Intimacy after Children

Overcoming the stumbling blocks to intimate relationship in marriage-with-children is challenging, but the challenge can be rewarding. Here are a few ways we can establish intimacy with our husbands.

* *Ask.* Ask your husband questions. Just a few at a time. Probing, curious questions. Interesting questions. What is his greatest dream in life? If he could do anything he chose with his time when he turns fifty, what would it be? What three adjectives would he like others to use in describing him?

    Ask questions you'd like to be asked. Questions that reflect your own curiosity. Questions that encourage him to be open, to share his dreams.

* *Listen.* After asking, listen. Open your ears and take in all you hear. Resist the urge to critique, redirect, evaluate. Just listen, accepting whatever you hear as having worth and value because it reflects something about the one you love.

"It is impossible to overemphasize the immense need people have to be listened to, to be taken seriously, to be understood," writes Paul Tournier. "No one can develop freely in this world and find a full life without feeling understood by at least one person."[16]

* *Act.* After asking and listening, put what you hear into action. Did you catch that tone in his voice—the one that says he's afraid you won't take him seriously? Will you grab that chance to compliment him in front of your friends?

Establish closeness in the little things. Lock eyes and wink from across a room. Share the buzz word or a private joke. Squeeze a hand when you're out in public. Blow a kiss through the window.

* *Risk.* It's not enough only to receive the shared soul of another person. If we want to establish intimate relationship with another, we must also take the risk to unveil who we are.

* *Adjust.* Marriages change. And they should, because the people in them change. As we invest in building a quality relationship, we must be open to adjusting ourselves within our relationships from time to time.

* *Forgive.* Anytime two people spend lots of time together, they are bound to irritate each other periodically with their quirky little habits, even those habits that seemed interesting or fun before marriage. "Opposites attract—until they get married" is a familiar saying. So we have to practice the art of forgiving. And the art of not holding grudges. "Keep short accounts," a pastor advised a soon-to-be-married couple, quoting

What Every **MOM** Needs

Scripture. "Do not let the sun go down while you are still angry" (Ephesians 4:26). Sure, we may need to give one another time to cool down and to process hurts or disagreements, but the habit of holding on to grudges becomes a brick wall to building intimacy.

Let's go back to a real-life marriage issue and apply these steps when two people are at completely different places sexually. (Marriage discussions always go back to sexual issues, don't they?)

Intimacy grows when we *ask* and *listen*. Take a few precious minutes before nodding off at night to talk together about what each of you is feeling and what you each need. Work at keeping up an intimate connection through communication even if the sexual side of intimacy isn't moving ahead at full steam. Acknowledge your husband's continuing desire while helping him understand your physical, emotional, and hormonal limitations. *Act* upon what you learn about each other, even if that means taking a *risk*.

Recognize together that this change in your feelings about your sex life won't be permanent. Make some *adjustments*, and *forgive* each other for not finding perfect solutions. With patience and continued care for one another, you can gradually move toward a mutually satisfying sex life.

Remember that, while a change in a couple's sex life is completely normal during the years of raising young children, sex is an important part of a marriage relationship. It is vital to experiencing the fullness of what marriage is intended to be. Don't give up on sex or write it off as a "has been" in your relationship.

Ask. Listen. Act. Risk. Adjust. Forgive. When you live this way, you're well on the road to building a deepening relationship with your spouse. It will require time and effort and intentionality, but the effort will strengthen and protect your relationship with your mate.

Extended Family Relationships

For many of us moms, our relationships with our own moms and dads and in-laws (now grandparents!) and grown siblings (aunts and uncles) are as integral to our lives as our friendships and our marriages. We may see them weekly or annually. They may be regular caregivers for our children or regular companions on shopping trips and outings with the kids or only occasional visitors. They may, in reality, be close friends as well as relatives.

Because they *are* relatives, though, these relationships also carry unique challenges. And as we enter life with children, these relationships often need to be renavigated just as friendships and marriages do when children enter the picture.

Our Parents

There is no one like Mom and Dad to delight in all the cute, funny, and new things our children do. We're likely to call them when that sign of a first tooth appears, when baby takes her first step, or preschooler arrives home from his first day of school.

But life with these now-grandparents may have its little, or big, kinks as well. Mom may not be as interested in our kids as we thought she would or should be. She may pressure us to call or come over more often than we're able. Dad might urge us to parent in ways we don't feel are best for our kids. Maybe he just isn't the positive "grandfather type" we want for our kids. Or maybe both spoil the kids with too many gifts or sweet treats.

On the other side of grandparenting are the in-laws. As in our other extended family relationships, our bond to our in-laws may range from wonderful to grisly. Relationships with in-laws can have added twists. They did things differently than our family did growing up. They have different holiday traditions, different philosophies on money and vacationing, different ideas on how to spend leisure time together, and different preferences regarding food and meals enjoyed together. Sometimes our relationships with these new family members can be colored by our differences. Opposing ideas on how to do things can get in the way of enjoying each other.

If you're married, make a conscious effort with your spouse to talk together about the areas that cause bumps in your relationship with his family. Make an effort to be open-minded. Consider how their way of doing things might be good too, even though it's different from yours. Decide which things are to be discussed with his family, and identify areas where both of you are agreed you can't bend as a family. Be gracious, loving, and firm when you communicate your needs to the in-laws. Do it together with your husband whenever possible. And remember, one of the best ways to love your husband well is to try to love his family well.

Make the most of this family who has been added to your life. For so many of us moms, these relationships can fill an important need in our lives and fill in holes that may not be filled by our own extended families.

No matter what their strengths and weaknesses as your parents and your kids' grandparents, they are a part of your life, and making the most of your relationships with them will benefit both you and your kids.

Let's remember:

- *They're learning too!* Just as we are learning every day as new mothers, our parents are learning too. They're learning to be Grandma and Grandpa and to let you be a parent rather than a dependent child. They'll make mistakes, just like you do.

- *They have limits just like you do.* Remember, they are older than you are and may have less energy for children than you do. Although many grandparents can almost run circles around younger moms, some find they're less able than they once were to manage the busyness of life with young children. Try to be conscious of who they are personality-wise, their energy level, and their desires as they relate to your children. Take what they can give and make the most of it.

- *They really have learned a few things in their time!* Some may be so concerned about giving too much advice that they don't offer any at all, while others seem to feel they should offer their views on every aspect of our parenting. And some relatives do a great job of finding a middle ground. Whatever style grandparents choose, let's keep in mind that they've been parents for many years, and they have learned things that can help us.

- *Grandparents are invaluable in your children's lives.* Grandparents play an important role in the life of your child. Your relationship with them is important for your kids' sake. Studies show that grandparents can play an integral role in the development of a child's sense of security and self-worth. And when children grow up relating to loving people in their lives who are older and have lived longer than their parents, they develop more depth and breadth as little people.

* *Let go of your ideals.* Sure, grandmas in books bake cookies with their grandchildren and sit by the fire reading them books. Maybe your mom, on the other hand, relies on Oreos and a super collection of kids' videos. You may have imagined your father taking your son fishing and he just doesn't ... but dwelling on your ideals won't change anything and won't do you much good. Focus, instead, on what they *are* giving to you and your kids and what you'd all miss if they weren't around.

Our Siblings

Some siblings may be much older and with kids in different stages, or much younger and without any kids at all. They may live near or far and be married or unmarried. Whatever their situation, a brother or sister provides the potential for filling an important place in our relationships. They understand your parenting background and share the family memories you carry into parenthood. They can encourage you like no other friend can. And they become aunts and uncles for life to your little ones.

We all need relationships. Whether in marriage, in friendship, or in extended families, we moms have a built-in longing for closeness. We want to be understood. We want the phone to ring. We need relationships, and when we recognize that desire and accept the responsibility to meet that need appropriately, we'll be better able to meet the needs of our children.

Mom Me Time

Mom Me Time 1
Friendship Tips

* *Busy Moms.* You're busy. So are your friends and potential friends. Schedule a date to go walking together, meet for coffee, or even just chat on the phone early in the morning or later in the evening, while kids are in bed. Plan several weeks or months ahead to spend a night or two away to scrapbook or just eat out and shop together. Take advantage of hotel specials during the off season. Take a class together. Strap on a phone headset and chat while folding laundry or cooking.
* *Single Friends.* With care, you can keep your single friends who don't have kids. Arrange for some kid-free time with your friend once in a while. Keep the conversation balanced — talk about more than your kids and family life. Spend time on your friend's turf occasionally.
* *When Children Conflict.* Work at keeping a friendship when your child has a conflict with a friend's child. Don't carry the battle to an adult level. Keep your friendship separate from the kids' friendship. Don't criticize her child or assign blame. Openly discuss the

issue and express your desire to remain close. Be pleasant to your friend's child.

* *Divorced or Widowed Friend.* When a close friend becomes a widow, separates, or divorces, listen well without feeling a need to comment or fix her feelings. Offer a specific form of help — "Can I mow the lawn?" Invite her to social activities but understand if she's not ready. Gently set boundaries for how much of her pain you can handle hearing about. Don't bash her ex-husband. Don't say, "You'll find someone else."

* *Newly at Home.* To make new friendships after quitting a job to be at home with kids, host a neighborhood coffee. Or plan dinner at a restaurant and invite the women on your block. Organize a Bunco night and invite neighbors. Attend a MOPS meeting nearby or a get-together with another moms' group.

* *Working and on the Go.* If you are working, whether full- or part-time, friendships can be the first to go. If this happens, you lose out. Stay in touch with friends through e-mail. Plan dates for your families to get together to "play." This way you see your friends and your kids have fun too. Try to squeeze in an occasional breakfast, dinner, or coffee date with a friend when the kids can be with Dad or Grandma. It's easy to forget about friendship in the rush of work and time with kids, so remind yourself to contact your friends with post-it notes, computer reminders, and photos of your friends nearby.

* *After a Move.* Seek out other newcomers through moms' groups, book clubs, or newcomers' clubs. Treat making friends like having a job. Be intentional in calling to

make coffee or play dates with potential friends. Don't take it personally when some women don't respond.

Mom Me Time 2
Strengthen Your Marriage Relationship!

Answering these questions will help you increase the level of intimacy in your marriage:

1. True or False: My husband and I maintain an active interest in each other's work life and friendships. We make an effort to keep up with names, problems, and job politics ongoing in the other's life.
2. True or False: My husband and I have made our marriage a priority above our relationship with our children.
3. True or False: We spend time alone each week.
4. True or False: My husband and I openly discuss our feelings about house rules for the children, spending, housework, and standards and values.
5. Think back to when you were dating. What sorts of things did you do then that you would like to do more of now? Write down three activities you could reinstate in your relationship.
6. When do you and your husband talk the most? (In the car, in the kitchen while cooking or doing dishes together, when you're out for dinner, after the kids go to bed?) Make the most of those situations and consciously use that time for talking.
7. List three things you could do to help your husband get more enjoyment out of his role as a dad.
8. List three little things you could do to improve the quality of the time you and your husband spend together.

What Every **MOM** Needs

9. How do you and your husband split up household and parenting responsibilities? Are you happy with this arrangement? What would you like to change?

10. What unrealistic expectations about marriage and parenting do you have, if any? You may need to discuss this with a friend to get another perspective.

11. What do you think are your husband's three biggest worries? Ask him, and see if you were right. What are your three biggest worries? Quiz your husband and see if he knows.

12. What do you think are your three biggest strengths as a wife? Ask your husband what he thinks they are, and compare. Conversely, decide what your husband's three greatest strengths are as a husband. Ask him what he thinks they are and once again, compare.[17]

Mom Me Time 3
Loneliness Busters

Take the initiative and try these when you're lonely:

* Call someone.
* Get physical. Take a walk. Clean a room.
* Be quiet. Turn loneliness into solitude with stillness.
* Be positive. Fight off the downward spiral of negativity. Count your blessings. Start a gratitude journal.
* Write an encouraging note to someone else.
* Be involved. The best cure for meeting a relationship need is to be a friend to someone else.
* Pray. Is there something God is trying to tell you right now, something you need to do or change?

Mom Me Time 4
Move Closer to Jesus

Be comforted and directed by these words written by Sister Basilea Schink: "The Lord in his love has planned pathways of loneliness for us, not so that our hearts will be tormented or embittered, but so that we shall seek him and draw closer to him."[18]

Mom We Time

Discuss these questions together, using the space on the following page to write your answers:

1. Can you identify with this chapter's discussion of loneliness? When in your life have you been most lonely? How "alone" have you felt in your loneliness — have you suspected that loneliness affects most women and specifically most mothers of young children?

    ----

2. If you are married, how has your friendship with your husband changed since you've had children? How has your romantic life with your husband changed since children?

    ----

3. How would you characterize your marriage in this season of your life?

    ❏ We're like Lucy and Ricky Ricardo of *I Love Lucy* — two hotheads and plenty of passion spent both in fighting and making up.
    ❏ We're more like Fred and Ethyl in *I Love Lucy* — I'm afraid we're becoming a cute old couple, complete with love handles around the middle!
    ❏ We're like Eric and Annie, or Mom and Dad, in *Seventh Heaven* — scrambling to keep up with the latest crisis of one of our kids while sneaking smooches behind momentarily closed doors.
    ❏ We're like Raymond and Debra in *Everybody Loves Raymond* — we laugh and tease a lot and do most of our talking propped up in bed at the end of the day.

❏ We could be the hosts of *Extreme Makeover: Home Edition*—it seems we don't do much more together than fix up our money pit of a home.

❏ I hate to say it, but we're like contestants on *Survivor*—sometimes we're on the same team pulling for each other in this crazy jungle of life, and other times all we do is accuse each other and bicker while we nurse our own wounds.

❏ Other:

4. How has a friendship in your life made a difference in your mothering and your overall outlook day to day? Share together about the way a friend has impacted your life.

_____

_____

_____

5. Now take a look around you. How well do you know each other? Would you call these women your friends? Each of us has something valuable to give one another in our lives as moms. Take a moment and try to identify together one strength of each woman in this group using these everyday comparisons. (You may want to have each item on hand and pass them out as you "award" each other.)

❋ *Super glue.* You work wonders when one of us is broken and hurting. You stand close and give the support that's needed to carry on with life.

❋ *Cooking spoon.* You have a real knack for helping people join together and form a bond even though they may be different from each other or complete strangers to begin with.

What Every **MOM** Needs

* *Child's scissors.* You have a way of carefully and gently cutting through the surface talk and getting down to deeper issues and real-life stuff that is going on with us. You help bring us closer together.
* *Whistling teapot.* You keep things bubbling when we spend time with you. You're full of energy and enthusiasm and always ready for a good time.
* *Scented candle.* You are quiet, but there is a strong flame inside you that is always burning for all of us to see. Just having you present when we're together adds a fragrance that calms us and pleases us.
* *Newspaper comics.* You always see the humorous side of things. You help us to lighten up and not take ourselves or our lives as moms so seriously.

Come up with your own if you'd like!

6. Now join with one woman sitting next to you and discuss together: If you were to identify one area of your relational life that needs some attention, what would it be? Your marriage? Your relationship with your mom? Your sister? A friendship that has drifted apart over time? A need for a new friend with a common interest or family situation? A plan for seeing your friends more regularly? A plan for deepening a friendship that has recently begun? Consider now how you can give this relationship some attention.

For Further Reading

Books

Relationships

Cloud, Henry, and John Townsend. *Boundaries: When to Say Yes, How to Say No to Take Control of Your Life.*

Hersh, Sharon. *Bravehearts: Unlocking the Courage to Love with Abandon.*

Kuykendall, Carol. *Five-Star Families: Moving Yours from Good to Great.*

Maxwell, John C. *Winning with People: Discover the People Principles That Work for You Every Time.*

Parrott, Les, III. *Coulda, Shoulda, Woulda: Live in the Present, Find Your Future.*

Rinehart, Paula. *Strong Women, Soft Hearts: A Woman's Guide to Cultivating a Wise Heart and a Passionate Life.*

Smalley, Gary. *The DNA of Relationships: Discover How You Are Designed for Satisfying Relationships.*

Marriage

Chapman, Gary. *The Five Love Languages: How to Express Heartfelt Commitment to Your Mate.*

Cloud, Henry, and John Townsend. *Boundaries in Marriage.*

Craker, Lorilee. *We Should Do This More Often: A Parents' Guide to Romance, Passion, and Other Pre-child Activities You Vaguely Recall.*

Dillow, Linda, and Lorraine Pintus. *Intimate Issues: Twenty-One Questions Christian Women Ask about Sex.*

What Every **MOM** Needs

Dobson, James. *Love for a Lifetime: Building a Marriage That Will Go the Distance.*

Eggerichs, Emerson. *Love and Respect: The Love She Most Desires, the Respect He Desperately Needs.*

Harley, Willard F., Jr. *His Needs, Her Needs for Parents: Keeping Romance Alive.*

Morgan, Elisa, and Carol Kuykendall. *Children Change a Marriage: What Every Couple Needs to Know.*

Parrott, Les, and Leslie Parrott. *I Love You More: How Everyday Problems Can Strengthen Your Marriage.*

———. *Love Talk: Speak Each Other's Language Like You Never Have Before.*

Smalley, Gary. *One Flame: How to Weather the Five Winds in Your Marriage.*

Thomas, Gary L. *Sacred Marriage: What If God Designed Marriage to Make Us Holy More Than to Make Us Happy?*

Friendship

Brestin, Dee. *The Friendships of Women: Harnessing the Power in Our Heartwarming, Heartrending Relationships.*

———. *We Are Sisters* (A sequel to the bestseller *The Friendships of Women*).

Laing, Kathleen, and Elizabeth Butterfield. *Girlfriends' Getaway: A Complete Guide to the Weekend Adventure That Turns Friends into Sisters and Sisters into Friends.*

Paul, Marla. *The Friendship Crisis: Finding, Making, and Keeping Friends When You're Not a Kid Anymore.*

Walker, Laura Jensen. *Girl Time: A Celebration of Chick Flicks, Bad Hair Days, and Good Friends.*

www.familylife.com. Led by Dennis and Barbara Rainey, national authors and speakers on marriage and family issues, familylife.com seeks to support marriages and families by providing resources for parenting and maintaining a healthy marriage. Through articles, a monthly e-magazine, discussion forums, and links to resources and books in an online store, Family Life touches on virtually every issue facing families today. Visitors can also listen to daily radio broadcasts and find out about how to attend Family Life speaking events and conferences locally. Familylife. com also offers sections that provide daily devotionals for couples, romantic ideas, and parenting tips.

www.marriagebuilders.com. Founded by Dr. Willard F. Harley Jr., Marriage Builders' main purpose is to educate couples about healthy marriages. This website provides basic concepts for a successful marriage, columns, and resources for frequently asked questions about common marriage problems with corresponding articles about each written by Dr. Harley. Guides to local seminars and workshops and a bookstore that provides full descriptions and a table of contents for each book sold round out the online resources. Marriage Builder home study courses are also available, complete with books and audio CDs. Perhaps the most impressive element on this site is access to a telephone counseling service. Site visitors can schedule an appointment with a counselor through a toll-free number and conduct sessions over the phone individually or as a couple.

www.realrelationships.com. Drs. Les and Leslie Parrott are a husband and wife counseling team based in Seattle. They have authored several books, independently and together, about relationships, including marriage and friendship, and are sought-after speakers. Their website offers information about nationwide seminars and conferences, marriage mentoring, and access to an online store where resources like books, workbooks, and videos can be purchased. Realrelationships.com also offers online relationship assessments and resources about conflict resolution that can be downloaded.

www.nationalmarriage.com. Information about choosing a great marriage counselor and information on intensive marriage counseling frame this website, which also offers articles for men and women about marriage and family issues. Information for couples, struggling marriages, and those in the premarital stage is available. Children's resources are also abundant, along with parenting information and a fiction selection in the online bookstore. Visitors can also stay updated with new articles and information offered on the site by signing up for an online newsletter delivered to their e-mail.

Four

Help

I Want Some Help!

*Many hands make light work,
and make the work a lot more fun!*

MomSpeak

* I think I need live-in help — day and night!

* There's not enough of me to go around! I'm a maid, cook, personal shopper, laundress, chauffeur, gardener, nurse, lover, teacher, organizer, professional in my field, and a playmate. What am I forgetting? Really, how does one person do it all?

* When my toddler fell on the fireplace hearth, I panicked! My husband was at work and we were new in the neighborhood. What else could I do? I grabbed a towel and my child and ran next door. Thank goodness, my neighbor was home! She bundled up her little one and raced me to the emergency room.

* I needed to go to the dentist. My mother couldn't take care of the kids. I was used to handling things on my own and didn't want to ask my friend. But I had to ... and she didn't mind at all.

* I realized I had to make a choice. Some moms keep a tight world. They don't ask for help and they don't offer help. They do life on their own. It doesn't make sense to me. I need help and I decided I want to get it and give it as much as I can.

What Every MOM Needs

W hat time are the Jacksons coming over tonight?" Tyler called to Mandy from his recliner in front of the TV, the remote control poised in his hand.

Tyler had just gotten home from work and looked beat. He'd been working too many long hours these days and he didn't expect much letup anytime soon. "Six o'clock," she called back as she rushed to put some bowls in the dishwasher. "In about ten minutes."

She looked forward to having the Jacksons over. Their kids were about the same ages and played well together, which gave the adults a chance to talk and have a little social life.

Mandy quickly took stock of her dinner preparations. The plates and silverware were set out buffet style and the meal was basically ready, but Legos still littered the family room floor. And a few stray, dried-up Play-Doh crumbs crunched under her feet as she stirred the soup and pulled the bread out of a bag to warm in the oven. Just then the children ran screeching from the bathroom to their bedrooms down the hall.

The bathroom. Oh no! She hadn't cleaned the bathroom yet. She peered across the room at Tyler, who was still changing channels. Covering the soup pot, she took long strides down the hall to the bathroom and flipped on the light. What a mess. Toilet paper hung from everywhere two feet high and under. Emily and Zach couldn't reach above that. The rest of the roll of paper floated in the toilet, which was surrounded by a big puddle of water. She heard giggles from behind the closed bedroom door down the hall.

Then the doorbell rang.

"Mandy! They're here!" Tyler yelled.

Grimacing, Mandy fished the wet roll of paper out of the toilet and threw it in the wastebasket. She reached for the hand towel, but it was missing. Then she spotted it—a wet wad stuck behind the toilet. *Murphy's law*, she thought to herself. *If anything can go wrong, it will!*

The doorbell rang again. The kids burst from their rooms and ran down the hall toward the front door, giggling and banging against the walls.

"Mandy! They're here! Are you going to get the door?" Tyler called again.

She felt the beginnings of mom fury churning inside. *He may be tired, but if he wants to see his friends, he could get out of the chair! And these little goofballs, they know better!*

"Hey—am I the *only* one who can answer the door? Am I the *only* one who can make dinner and clean up and watch the kids?" As Mandy scooped up the towel from behind the toilet, she realized that something was going to have to change. "Hey—does anyone out there realize I could use some help? I said, *help!*"

A Mom's Confession: "I Need Help!"

When mothers of preschoolers were asked, "What do you need most?" they offered a smattering of answers:

* A housekeeper
* A nanny
* A secretary
* Another set of arms
* To get organized
* Help

Many moms answered, "Time!" which translates into "Help!" Other moms described the difference between expectations and reality. "I find myself screaming and getting frustrated and I know that's not what I'm supposed to be doing," said one mom. "Sometimes I feel like I'm losing my mind. I need help!"

"My husband is actually a lot of help with the kids and the house," said one married mom. "But the truth is that I still carry the bulk of the load at home." Another mom, asked when she recognized her need for help, simply answered, "Mommy, Mommy, Mommy, Mommy, Mommy, *Mommy!*"

While we might blurt out confessions like these, when it comes down to everyday life, most of us go to great lengths on our own before actually asking for help. Griping comes more easily. We whine, and then when pushed to the brink, we explode by yelling. Or crying, as this mom describes, "My husband had been traveling a lot for his job, and I was alone with the kids most of the time. A policeman pulled me over for speeding, and I broke down. That ticket was just one more thing I would have to take care of! I sobbed and sobbed with my head down on the steering wheel. The policeman, I think feeling sorry for me, let me go with a warning." And many of us have mastered the martyr role, in which we carry on our work while sighing frequently and loudly, in hopes that someone will notice our weariness and step in to help. But when it comes to asking for specific assistance, we don't do it.

Why? Because we tend to feel that asking for help is a sign of helplessness or weakness, and we are determined not to be weak. As women, we've made the choice to be mothers, and now we will deal with whatever motherhood throws our way, we reason. When a broken toy is tearfully brought to us, we superglue it back together. When a favorite "tickle tag" falls off a blankie, we sew it back on. When the chocolate chip cookies are gone, we bake—or buy—some more. When the milk spills, we clean it up. It doesn't occur to some of us to enlist help until we absolutely, positively need it or have run completely out of energy to manage anymore.

Why do we avoid getting help? We feel *guilty* about asking for help. Just admitting that we can't do it all and could use some help feels like admitting failure. Call your sister to take the baby for a couple hours so that you can sleep and get over your cold? Ask a neighbor to pick up your son from preschool so you can take the baby to the doctor? Ask a friend to keep your child for a play morning so that you can make an early morning meeting? *Well, is there any other way?* we ask ourselves.

Then we look at a neighbor friend, who has two more kids than we do, what seems like a clean house all the time, and she always looks great and put together. *If she can do it, then certainly I should be able to*, we muse. And again we begin to feel guilty that we aren't handling things a lot better than we think we should be.

Mothers of preschoolers don't have occasional guilt. We have "perma-guilt" that sticks closer to us than our push-up bras and cotton undies. If we can't be everything for our families, we may as well throw in the towel (while we're doing the laundry anyway) and admit failure, we tell ourselves. As much as we'd like to have some help and desperately need help, we refrain from actually asking for it.

But No One Offers to Help!

Maybe you're a single mom and it's all you can do just to get the kids to day care, handle the day's work, and then get them back home and fed again in the evening. Or maybe you're married but your husband works long hours, travels all week, works nights, or simply doesn't get what kind of help you need. As this mom describes: "When my two-year-old son is screaming because he can not drink my perfume and my baby is wanting to breast-feed *right now* and can't because I am now cleaning up my favorite perfume from the kitchen floor and my mother is calling repeatedly leaving messages wanting to know why I have not picked up the phone ... In comes Dad to save the day, sees I am upset, and wants to jump on my bandwagon and decides to punish my son for a reason which he does not know. So I have to calmly explain that the child has already had a time-out and that I need him to be patient now because I can not be anymore. Meanwhile my baby is now feverishly sucking her fist and has just pooped all over the only clean shirt I have left."

Or maybe your husband simply isn't interested in helping parent and run the household. "Help? Are you kidding? No one's breaking down my door to come in and help," you laugh. "Everybody I know has the same problem I do. Who has time to help?"

It's true — often we look around us and see our friends and extended family dealing with the same challenges we are. They have kids and jobs and busy lives. They don't have any more time or energy than we do, so why would we look to them for help? And then we get so used to handling everything on our own, it doesn't even occur to us to ask for help.

Think outside the Box

Sometimes we don't think long enough or far enough outside of our little worlds. Often we can find help, willing and capable help, if we can just get a little creative. Even the busy people in our lives often have room and enjoy helping if we can find the ways that work for their lives. The Bible encourages us to turn to others, so we have good reason to explore all the options. "Two are better than one, because they have a good return for their labor: If they fall down, they can help each other up. But pity those who fall and have no one to help them up!" (Ecclesiastes 4:9 – 10 TNIV).

Who can you turn to for help in your parenting? When you do, there's a good chance your child will enjoy the change of pace as much as you do.

Your best friend and your husband, if you're married, are obvious possibilities. Have you asked them? How about your doctor? Would he or she be able to suggest a solution to a problem you are facing or point you to a helpful resource? How about your child's preschool teacher? Maybe she would love to have your child for the afternoon sometime or could suggest some ways you could keep him busy while you work at home. How about sharing cooking with a neighbor or two — you cook one night for everyone; they cook another night. Do you need a homeschooling network group? You don't have to go it alone. What about a babysitter? A babysitting co-op? Does a friend have a child who's reached babysitting age? Are there kids who babysit at your church or in your neighborhood? How about your next-door neighbor? A grandmother?

From extended family to the friends who have become your chosen family, to community and church resources, you have partners in parenting. As a mom you may always be "on duty," but you, and your kids, will live better when you partner with others to share the responsibility.

You've heard the African proverb, "It takes a village to raise a child." Yes, it does. We know it and so does our friend, author Carla Barnhill. She writes, "A friend once asked me if I believed 'all that "it takes a village" bunk.' Absolutely! Without a connection to other women, to other roles, to other passions, a woman becomes a shell of who she was created to be."[1] So find the help. It *is* out there, and both you and your child will benefit when you ask.

Girlfriends to the Rescue!

What would we do without our girlfriends? We need them in our life for coffee breaks, Bunco nights, early morning exercise, trips to the zoo with ten kids in tow, and heartfelt encouragement that yes, we can make it through one more pregnancy, even if it is another set of twins. We need our friends for more than companionship, though. We need them to be a big part of "the village" for us and our kids.

Mom and author Donna Partow confesses this slow but sure discovery, "This motherhood trip wasn't designed for lone rangers. It takes more than one woman against the world to raise a child in this increasingly complex and dangerous world. Even the pioneers sometimes circled the wagons. Women need one another. It's time to circle the wagons."[2]

One-on-One Help

When you finally get up the nerve to ask a friend for help, you may be pleasantly surprised by the response.

The result of receiving help one-on-one outweighs the risk of asking. In fact, many long-lasting friendships between women begin this way. Have you realized that when you ask a friend to watch your kids for you, or give you a ride when your car won't start, or share some recipes for quick and easy meals, you are giving her the permission to ask for your help sometime? In a way, you're giving her an IOU and the freedom to use it. Of course, we don't need to keep an even score in helping each other, but we're all human in our desire to give as well as receive. If you get the ball rolling, both you and your friend will be grateful. You'll also have a lot more connections with each other in which you can talk and laugh and become better friends.

Can't Pay? Then "Barter" for Help!

Bartering is an old-fashioned term to describe task trading. Have you found someone who can do a job you can't? Bartering is a great way to receive the help you need without spending the money you don't have. Bartering also makes it possible to spend more time on what you enjoy doing while letting someone else do what you don't enjoy.

Do you need a room painted but have no idea what color to choose, what paint to buy, or where to begin? Call up that neighbor who not only paints, but does faux finishes, murals, and window treatments too. Offer to babysit, cook meals, make hand-stamped cards, or whatever you do, in return for her help. Maybe you like a clean home but can't manage to get down and really scrub with your little ones underfoot. You can't afford a cleaning lady or a babysitter on a regular basis, so find a friend with the same problem and swap kids two days a week, or even two days a month. Maybe you and a friend both work part-time at home. Try to coordinate your work schedules so that you can care for each other's kids and get more done in less time. The possibilities are unlimited. One mom with six kids and an extremely tight budget says she barters for everything from haircuts to furniture and cars to Christmas presents for her kids. Let's get wheeling and dealing, moms!

Join a Group

Whether or not you consider yourself a "groupie" kind of girl, now is the time to give groups a try. We need our friends, but there is also nothing like being part of something bigger.

Journalist Marla Paul admits, "Plenty of us are reluctant joiners." She tells of many groups she quit over the years, feeling they just weren't her. But when she moved to a new city, none of her relationships seemed like enough. "I didn't know that I was missing community." She quotes psychologist Belle Liang: "Hanging out with a gang, in some ways, is even more important for women than individual friendships.... There is something about being in a group that helps people to feel more of an equilibrium. In some ways, while you gain your identity, you also lose your identity and become part of something bigger than yourself, less of a self-consciousness and more of a collective focus. It really grounds a person."[3]

Another mom shares her experience: "I first came to MOPS (Mothers of Preschoolers) when a friend invited me. As I sat there with that group of women, I thought to myself, *How pathetic. I'm at a support group. Have I really sunk this low?* After that first meeting, I realized it was much more. It was great to learn in all different areas and to help solve problems by sharing with other women."

There are lots of groups you could join or start to meet all sorts of needs. Set up a children's playgroup or a babysitting co-op. Go online for tips on how to start one, and then enjoy regular dates with your husband or kid-free time to do what you need. Consider a food co-op to get discount prices on large quantities. Join a support group on parenting issues where you can gather with others struggling with the same questions and concerns. Time with people in person is a must, but even online support groups or chat rooms can offer real and readily available help for a specific issue you are dealing with.

Have a Heart-to-Heart with Your Man

If you're married, the most obvious source of help is your husband! But *expecting* help from him may be another matter altogether. There are of course many men who help out as if they were *born* to load and unload the dishwasher, fold the laundry, and pick up toys. Great modeling from their own moms and dads prepared them well!

But often—as much as we love our men—it seems that sometimes their intentions just don't get off the ground, for lots of reasons. One mom says, "I'm married but sometimes feel like a single mom because my husband works twelve to fourteen hours a day, six days a week."

If we don't make our needs known, others just don't get a clue that we need help. Another mom says, "My kids place their food and drink orders all day. My husband stays after work to have a beer, comes home, eats, and goes to bed. I feel like no one thought of me at all the whole day."

And some men don't understand the kind of help we need. "When the kids whine and cry, my husband tells me not to let them get to me. He tells me what to do, instead of helping with them."

Lots of husbands face the same issues we do. They are stretched at work with too much to do in too little time, and they may have outside commitments. As women, we're quick to sympathize with their needs for rest and downtime. But it leaves us in the same place, with no help! One mom explained, "Sometimes I feel myself hitting my limit and know I need some help. I realize I need to ask for help and not feel bad about it, but I find it difficult to ask, especially when my husband has had a long week at work."

And what about the issue of roles? What is the mom's job and what is the dad's? How do we sort through who does what? Does playtime for Daddy and kids take priority over household chores? One mom voiced her feelings. "My husband comes home and my son wants Daddy. They play and have fun, and I feel invisible. I feel like I work all the time — if not with my son, then in the house. When my husband comes home from work, his job is done and playtime starts."

Then there are the times we ask for help, and we get no response. So rather than raise an issue, we do it ourselves. "One typical Saturday I needed to watch both kids, clean and vacuum, do the dishes and laundry, get dinner, and still find time to relax with my husband. It didn't work because he wouldn't help out. So I ended up doing everything myself," said a mom.

Many of us have husbands who do help and who realize that running the house and parenting the kids is not the woman's sole responsibility. These guys are great. Many of us, though, can still see room for improvement in the whole parenting partnership. Needs change with every child, with every change in jobs for either spouse, and even as kids grow and enter new stages. So don't feel your husband is a louse or your teamwork is a failure just because it's not working quite like it should.

Talk about Your Parenting Partnership

Authors Karol Ladd and Jane Jarrell remind us that we're not doing ourselves or our family any favors if we don't address our needs. "First, take a good long look at your parenting expectations. Expectations that do not mesh with reality become a breeding ground for discontent. Discontent can color your world in shades you never thought possible. If you find your home life to be less than satisfactory, stop and reflect on this area of your relationship with your husband."[4]

Who should do what around the house? Does it work best for you both to define clearly who does what, or do you work better together with a "divide and conquer" game plan that you work out on a daily or weekly basis? How should parenting time be handled when both parents are home? When one or the other is working? What about when one of you is sick, what should be expected? What kind of models do you want your children to take with them into their own marriages some day?

Plan dinner out or a quiet time with Starbucks and a special dessert at home to hash through these issues specifically and sensitively. Let your husband know how important this kind of talking is to you. You'll be happier as a mom and a wife if you feel like he's your partner and not just another child to take care of. Everyone will be happier. As we all know, "If Mama ain't happy, ain't nobody happy!"

Writing on becoming strong as a woman, Ruth Barton says:

The most encouraging thing that has happened for me as a mother is that Chris (my husband) and I have begun seeing ourselves more clearly as a team in this challenge-of-a-lifetime called parenting. I have found that I do not need another book on how to be a better mother.... What I have needed is my husband, the father of these children, to participate more fully with me in this great call of God upon our lives. I have needed to hear him say with words and with action, "You are not alone. These children are just as much my responsibility as they are yours."[5]

Dad Will Never Be Mom — and That's Okay

Research shows that mothers and fathers parent in different ways and are able to provide for unique needs in their children. Whereas the mother is the primary source of attachment, so necessary for infant bonding and future social relationships, the father is the main source for increasing the child's physical and intellectual independence. Infants value their fathers' "optimally novel stimuli." They are not so unfamiliar as to provoke stranger anxiety, but they come and go often enough to stimulate interest as "exciting novelties."[6]

Developing a co-parenting style takes work and patience. It requires honest self-examination and careful communication.

Take an honest look at your parenting style. If you're running the family ship like the captain of the fleet, issuing orders and demanding compliance, you may be able to enjoy a sense of control, but you won't see help coming forth from your husband. A willingness to help comes from a shared sense of ownership of responsibility. Are your children *your* children or are they your husband's children as well?

Think about it. What's your "MO" — your modus operandi or method of handling life with husband and kids? Do you leave detailed lists about how to diaper, feed, and play with the baby when you leave for a girls' night out? Or do you let your husband figure out what works for him? When he's on duty for a morning or an evening with the kids, do you remind him the day before that he'll be *babysitting* or simply on his own with the kids? Even subtle words like these can communicate that what he is doing as a father is as meaningful as what you do as a mother. If we want our men to be all they can be as dads and husbands, let's be consistent in what we expect and in the language we use to talk about it. And let's admit that sometimes we may be part of the problem and may also need to work at doing some things differently.

Men Don't Read Minds — So Ask!

Once you've had "the big talk" about who you want to be as parents and how you want to keep your household at least reasonably orderly and efficient, accept that your work isn't done. Expect a continuing need for good communication and a process that will take time for both of you.

You'll need to:

* *Ask clearly and directly.* Don't hint. Don't sigh or pout. Don't expect him to read your mind or even notice your needs. We may feel, "I shouldn't need to tell him. He should just *know* and do it." Well, reality is, sometime they don't. Let's get rid of what would be ideal, and just accept that we need to spell it out. Tell him. Put your request in words.

"I need help with the house. Would you please do the vacuuming?" "I need to go to the mall without having to spend a half hour at the fountain throwing pennies and another half hour chasing Ellie out from under the racks of clothes. I need you to do something with her while I'm gone for a couple of hours." "I need help with the grocery shopping this week. The baby screams all the way through the store and I don't have the energy to handle that. Can you stop there after work and get what we need?"

Maybe you don't often ask for this kind of help. *Now is the time to start!* Life with kids won't get easier. Different, but not easier. As we said before, you'll *all* be happier if you begin asking now and get some new patterns developing in your family life. Ask when you're calm and can foresee a need so that you don't explode in anger later when you're at the end of your rope. When that happens, getting and receiving the help is a lot more difficult.

✳ *Live with the results.* If you ask your husband to vacuum, resist the urge to critique his work. If you ask him to take Ellie while you shop, then embrace his choices as to what he does with her while you're away. If you send him to the grocery store, enjoy the "extras" he gets when he returns.

If you want help, receive what you're given. He may not do it exactly as you would, but being critical won't do anything to help build the partnership you're looking for.

* *Take a risk.* It feels risky to change a pattern of relating or communicating in a marriage. If your guy has grown accustomed to your being a "Supermom" with the kids and "Superwoman" in general, he may have a hard time adjusting to a new reality. Give him time. Remind him often that you'll have more to give him and the kids if you're getting the help you need.

  Of course, all of your requests for help won't meet with backflips and immediate action. He may just flat out say no. Expect it and receive it without wasting a lot of emotional energy on a response. After all, *you* need to say no to him at times too. But don't stop asking.

Ask clearly. Live with the results. Be willing to risk. And understand that true partnership in parenting grows out of a deepening relationship. When you are investing ongoing nurture in your marriage relationship, you can learn to ask for the help you need, and he can learn to offer it.

Mommy's Little Helpers

If they're not babies, do you get your children to help?

That's a loaded question, you may be thinking. "To tell you the truth, it's easier to do it myself," most of us may reply. Either their ears happen to have difficulty hearing when we ask them and nagging just gets too tedious, or they end up making more work for us in helping than we would have had without their help.

Sometimes reverse psychology works — we know well the truth in that wall hanging we've all seen: "There are three ways to get something done: Do it yourself, hire someone, or forbid your kids to do it."

Still, we *can* work at training our little ones, even now, to be our helpers. There are certainly some chores, like mopping the floor and cleaning the mirrors, that they actually think are fun.

It's for Their Own Good – and Ours!

If you shudder at the thought of teaching your three-year-old to help put clothes in the washer or put the silverware away, think of it this way: When he gets his first apartment, will he pull his silverware from a silverware drawer, or will he just use it straight from the basket in the dishwasher? When he's in college, will he know when washing clothes to separate whites from darks and that if you put too many clothes in the dryer they wrinkle and never completely dry?

Maybe you have a brother who still, at age thirty-five, doesn't know how to wash a load of clothes or fix a pot of spaghetti. Even some of us moms had to learn as adults, the hard way, how to clean toilets and mop floors and brown hamburger because our mothers never involved us in the chores around the house.

"My mom thought she was letting me have a carefree childhood," said one mom. "She did all the cooking and cleaning by herself. But the reality was, the house was never clean and the home-cooked meals were only sporadic. Then I had to take a crash course in 'happy homemaking' and teach myself these skills far away in another state after college. I wish I'd learned more from my mom."

Sure, we can't expect our little ones to learn it all now, but now is the time to start. Cooking, cleaning, and washing clothes are skills that are best taught by instruction and repetition. A child doesn't automatically begin to exercise these skills when he or she turns eighteen. We help them out by beginning to teach them now (before they become moody teenagers!). Not only will it make their lives easier as adults, but it will also influence who they become as grown people, for their families and for the larger world they inhabit.

It makes our world at home better too. Imagine—coming home to find the dinner table all ready. Or seeing a toddler make her bed without being reminded. Imagine climbing into a bathtub that was cleaned after the last use. Or returning to a kitchen where cereal bowls have been stacked in the sink or put in the dishwasher instead of left on the table, surrounded by puddles of milk! This kind of help makes a huge difference in a mom's life. Just knowing our kids are learning to help energizes us to keep on keeping on.

Help Your Children Help

Obviously, we can't expect much in the way of help from children under the age of two. But even toddlers can begin to "help Mommy" with small tasks.

* *Select age-appropriate tasks for your children.* Ask the younger ones to put away plastic containers, pick up their toys, or put their dirty clothes in the hamper. In this stage of developing independence, these kinds of chores can actually assist their need to do things "all by myself." Increasing their responsibilities as they grow older will keep them motivated and challenged.
* *Motivate kids with rewards.* Whether it's verbal praise, an allowance, a treat, or something else you feel is appropriate, motivate your children to be helpers. Be sure

What Every **MOM** Needs

to withhold rewards until tasks are complete, because this way you teach them about the logical consequences of their actions. Once the tasks are satisfactorily completed, give the rewards with gusto!

* *Adjust your standards of a job well done.* Children will often mess up more than they clean up as they begin the helping process. Steel yourself during these days. Bite your tongue and forbid your hands from straightening the bedspread or moving the salad fork to its proper slot! Your response to initial efforts will set the tone for future attempts. If a child feels unsuccessful, he or she may not want to risk further failure. Reward the effort and the attitude more than the perfection of the task completed.

With patience and persistence, mommy's little helpers can grow into mom's capable crew.

Help for Moms with Extra Challenges

Every mom needs help. Some of us need it because we are dealing with big challenges like single parenting, a special needs child, multiples (twins, triplets), a child who is seriously ill, or the grief of miscarriage, infertility, or a child who has died. These challenges can be all consuming and can shut down many of the other parts of our lives because of the energy and focus that is required to deal with our situation.

You *do* need help, Mom, and you may continue to need help for a while. Make a decision right now to drop the guilt and accept that you are just one person with limited time, energy, resources, and emotional capacity. You need help, and that's okay. You probably even need help *finding* help. Accept the help that is offered and make a habit of asking for it when it's not. Think carefully about what your needs are, and then be specific with others. Often those who may want to help just don't know what to do.

Connect with support groups that cater to your particular situation, and take advantage of all they have to offer. Other moms with similar challenges will likely be your biggest source of support. They are or have been where you are, and when we moms link arms to conquer especially difficult challenges, we form a bond that is life-changing.

Free Yourself to Ask for Emotional Help

Maybe you read the title of this chapter and thought, "Yes, please tell me there are other moms out there who wonder if they're losing their mind, or can't seem to shake a major bummed-out feeling, or just can't seem to connect with life or people much anymore. Tell me how I can get some *help*, because I think I might need some *serious* help!"

If you can relate, maybe your need for help goes deeper than a need for a clean bathroom or reliable child care. You may need help sorting through your feelings. You may need help determining if you're suffering depression. You may need help in the form of medication to regulate a chemical imbalance in your body. Depression is more common than you might suspect, and yet it's not talked about much. Most women who are suffering depression don't know it and haven't even considered the possibility.

Carla Barnhill, an author who shares about her own experience with depression, says, "It never occurred to me that I was experiencing anything other than a normal reaction to life as a busy, tired woman."[7] Yet her symptoms fit what might be termed "high-functioning depression." Dr. Archibald Hart and his daughter, Christian psychotherapist Catherine Hart Weber, write, "Mothers have to deal with a constant flow of pressures and the 'chronic strain of the mundane,' everyday home management, baby nurturing, and toddler parenting, not to mention the care of teenagers and husbands.... These demands are all part of modern life, and they don't necessarily lead to clinical depression. That doesn't mean we should underestimate their effects. The cumulative outcome of trying to survive while keeping up with the rest of the human race, with no opportunity for respite, can lead to a devastating depression."[8]

You might want to do some research on depression. Could it be affecting you? Here is a summary of what women may experience with depression:

* Difficulty getting through a daily routine
* Sleeping too much or too little
* Disturbance of concentration
* Excessive negativity or pessimistic thoughts
* Severe guilt
* An inability to connect with or be around others
* Feelings of being overwhelmed, anxious, worthless, and hopeless

If you think you may be experiencing depression, talk to your gynecologist, or a professional counselor, or at the least a sensitive friend who may be able to point you toward good help. Larger churches often offer free counseling services, and there are good books that will help you better identify and deal with depression (see resources at the end of this chapter). Studies on depression show that usually medication alone is not sufficient for treating depression. The combination of medication and counseling usually proves most effective. Don't feel that exploring and admitting to this problem labels you as weak or problematic. Statistics show that probably one in five women deal with depression at some point in their lives.[9] You have company, and with good help and understanding, you can move toward better, brighter days.

Whether you are suffering from depression or just feeling a bit fragile emotionally, stop looking around and comparing yourself to the other moms around you. Comparison is probably the biggest "zapper" of our self-image as mothers and of our joy in mothering. Sure, someone else makes an annual gingerbread house with her kids and always has her family Christmas photo card out on time. Another friend has a home that could appear in a magazine, and your sister is teaching her toddler to speak French. Resist that maddening tendency to equate good mothering with a good show of outward accomplishment. We all excel in different areas of motherhood. Much of what we require of ourselves as moms—and use in comparisons with others—is of little consequence or ultimate necessity to children. *You* are the best and most qualified mother for your children for very good reasons. Sure, you may struggle more than another mother in some area, but you're also more capable at something else.

The Ultimate Helper

Last, but certainly not least, we can find the most help of all in God, who is always available to us and always able. The book of Psalms gives this promise: "God is our refuge and strength, an ever-present help in trouble" (Psalm 46:1). We'll talk more about the help we can find in God later in the book. For now, we'll just say that God is first on the list when it comes to seeking help. And he created us as dependent people who need each other—and him.

Help is there for you, Mom. But getting help begins by connecting with the people in your life and asking for it. The risk is worth the reward, for everyone involved. So reward yourself, Mom, and get some help!

Mom Me Time

Mom Me Time 1
Help Me Get Organized!

It comes with the territory—mothering and that nagging feeling that you need to be better organized. Moms Karol Ladd and Jane Jarrell have formed a club for those moms who flit from one task to another and feel prone to *dis*organization: Hummingbird Heads Anonymous. Do you qualify? Take this test.

- ❏ You find yourself disorganized despite tremendous intentions.
- ❏ You are pile challenged.
- ❏ Your car has last week's Happy Meal in the backseat. Okay, let's be honest. It probably has last year's Happy Meal and fries lodged under the backseat.
- ❏ On your way to the store you forget what you need to buy.

- You own more than five books on the topic of organization.
- Your hair stands on end when around the overtly organized.
- You pay late fees for library books and videotapes on a regular basis.
- You can be a lot of fun.
- You enjoy gooey snacks rich in fat, especially halved with other HHA members.
- Right this moment you do not know where your car keys are.

If you can answer yes to at least seven of these items, then welcome to the flock, sister![10]

Here are just a few tips from mom Cathy Penshorn for staying organized:

* Experiment with different kinds of toy containers and shelving systems. Toys need to be *easy* for kids to put away or it won't happen.
* Have a small table or shelf for "in progress" games and projects, like Lego, K'Nex, or Bionicle creations. Anything they want to work on over time can go there.
* Have an "odds and ends" bucket, basket, or box for yourself that you can toss things into over the course of the day. Have one child play delivery person at the end of the day to put the items in their appropriate spots.
* Use a vertical file divider at a desk or counter to hold bills, correspondence, school papers, sport schedules, coupons, and miscellaneous.
* Keep cleaning supplies in each bathroom so that you save time by not running around the house when cleaning.[11]

Talk to other moms, look for books at your library, and find resources on the Internet to help you organize in the areas you need. We've learned that, over time, most moms develop systems that work reasonably well for their families' needs. And as kids grow, it gets a little easier. Take it in stride, Mom, and don't expect too much of yourself!

Mom Me Time 2
Help in Finding Quality Child Care

At some point all moms with preschoolers come face-to-face with the need to find quality child care. Whether it's sporadic or ongoing regular care you need, the same principles apply. Look for:

* *A Shared Set of Common Values.* Will your child care provider support the values you want to instill in your child? Do you hold the same view of TV watching? Will the discipline be consistent with what you do at home? Asking pointed questions of potential caregivers and their references will help you determine who will most consistently follow the beliefs and standards you hold dear.

* *Flexibility.* Look for someone who is willing to accommodate your needs and schedule and work with your child, taking into account your child's individual bent or personality. Honestly communicate your needs and expectations, and then listen carefully to their responses.

* *Communication Skills.* Knowing what's happening with your child is important. Look for someone willing to share openly what happened when your child was away

from you. What did your child do? Were there any unusual behaviors? Did something special happen? Ask questions and expect answers!

* *Daily Routine.* If your child needs regular day care, ask about the daily routine that is followed (playtime, snacks, lunch, nap). Will the children go on field trips or outings away from the home or day care center? If so, how is transportation handled?

* *Cleanliness.* How well is the home or facility cleaned or sanitized? Ask about the standards and inspect for yourself.

* *Commitment to Safety.* Knowing that your precious child is in safe hands gives you peace of mind and lets you enjoy your time away. Child care providers should take your child's safety seriously. Look for possible safety hazards. Is the primary focus your child, or are the providers easily distracted? What do they consider to be age-appropriate activities for your child? Accidents can and do happen, but look for a conscientious attitude.

* *Consistency.* Look for someone you can count on regularly, rather than a myriad of different babysitters. Familiarity builds trust and security in children.

The options are varied: at-home care or away; teenage babysitters, college students, or older adults; babysitting co-ops where moms trade hours, or Mom's Day Out preschool programs. For recommendations, ask family members or close friends and neighbors. Check with a church, your own or another nearby. Get the opinions of other parents. Visit and ask questions. Always consider what is best for your child.

Take your time, be observant, and trust your own instincts, your child's responses, and God's guidance.

Mom Me Time 3
Chores for Kids

Invest in your most obvious and constant helpers with these suggestions for preschoolers. Patricia Sprinkle lists these age-appropriate tasks in her book *Do I Have To?*

Tasks for Two- and Three-Year-Olds

* load spoons into dishwasher
* help feed animals
* put away toys after play
* wipe table
* dry unbreakable dishes
* sweep (small broom)
* wipe mirrors (parent sprays)
* entertain infant
* bring in newspaper
* dress and undress
* mop small area
* pour milk (small pitcher)
* empty wastebaskets
* dig and pull weeds in garden
* dust furniture
* fold dishtowels
* put away silverware
* load washer, unload dryer
* stir orange juice
* assist with stirring in cooking
* brush teeth, wash face
* tidy magazines, sofa pillows
* pick up trash in yard
* set table (from diagram)

Additional Tasks for Four- and Five-Year-Olds

* put away own clothes
* clean mirrors and glass alone
* hang towels after bath
* plant seeds
* sort clean laundry

* set a complete table
* clean bathroom sinks
* help with simple desserts
* help load dishwasher
* take dirty clothes to hamper

* carry own dishes to sink
* mix salads
* put away groceries
* sort wash loads by color
* bring in the mail and put in proper place[12]

Cleaning Games for Preschoolers

1. *Colors and Shapes.* Say to your child, "Let's pick up all the red toys. Now let's pick up all the blue ones." "Let's pick up all the squares and rectangles. Now the toys with round parts." "Let's put all the glasses into the dishwasher. Now let's put in all the plates."

2. *Observer Game.* Say, "You put away ten things and let's see if I can remember them in order. Maya put away a ball. Maya put away a ball and a truck. Maya put away a ball, a truck, and a doll."

3. *Dust Muppet or Monster.* Draw a face on a large white sock for a dust mitt that "eats" dust.

4. *Family Army Game.* Put on march music. Line up at attention, then march around the room picking up toys and putting them away in time to the music. When done, report back to the "General" (parent or older child) and salute.

5. *Ant Legion.* Read Proverbs 6:6 and talk about how hard ants work, then pronounce everyone an ant. The ants work hard and fast to see how quickly they can clean a room.

6. *Do It with Me.* Say, "You make one side of the bed and I'll make the other." "You vacuum the room while I dust it." "You clean the mirror while I clean the toilet." Tell jokes while you work together.

7. *Surprise Me!* Leave the room after asking the child to see how much she can get done before you return. Pop right back in and say, "I was just teasing this time, but you don't know when I'll be back next time, do you?" Return when you think the job may be done.

8. *"This Is the Way We . . ."* Remember that old song? Sing together as you do the chore. How many times do you have to sing it before the job is done?

9. *Go Shopping.* Fill a wagon, buggy, or box with toys to be put away, pretending you are shopping, "Oh, I think I'll buy this bear. What will you buy?"

10. *Beat the Clock.* Agree to work ten minutes. Set a timer.[13]

How to Teach a Child a Skill

1. Be familiar with the skill you are going to teach.
2. Develop a logical way to present it.
3. Take kids with you to get materials so they will be able to find them alone later.
4. Name what you are going to teach.
5. Give kids your full attention.
6. Present the lesson carefully and precisely.
7. Use no more language than is necessary.
8. In general, move from left to right.

9. Let your children join in the tasks as soon as they are ready.
10. If they make a mistake, don't draw attention to it.
11. Stay with the kids until you are sure they can work alone.
12. Allow them to work as long as they wish at this new skill.[14]

Mom Me Time 4
Tips for Single Moms

Single moms face some issues and challenges that are different from those of two-parent families. Such issues include dealing with finances and facing a greater need for partners in parenting.

For financial advice contact Crown Financial Ministries (for books, tapes, and booklets) at www.crown.org.

To find other partners in parenting, here are some suggestions:

1. Become involved in a church that understands and ministers to single parents—one that includes singles in their family activities and sponsors care groups that involve people in all situations. Although a singles group is good for some of your social needs, you also need to develop relationships with couples in the church.
2. Look to the church and your family for healthy male role models for your kids. Take the time to pray and watch. Observe some of the fathers in your church to see who handles discipline and fun

well. Choose someone who honors his wife and his children. Ask the couple if it would be all right to take one or more of your children along on some family functions. Maybe the family would include your children on a fishing or ski trip. Explain your kids' need to experience a healthy Christian family with a strong male role model.

3. It's important for you to get as much help as you can in raising your kids. Make sure you have a woman mentor. As a single mom, you have a pressing need to be able to discuss parenting issues with someone. Who better than someone who has been there before and can share her experience with you? Work with an older woman who can become a friend, someone who is sensitive and has been successful as a mother — someone you can confide in. If possible, look to someone who has had more than one child and understands different temperaments and discipline issues.[15]

Some single moms find help by reaching out to their married friends who are more than willing to share their husbands as helpers in a pinch.

For further resources:

* Parents without Partners, 1650 South Dixie Highway, Suite 510, Boca Raton, FL 33432; (561) 391-8833; www.parentswithoutpartners.org. This is the largest organization devoted to the welfare and interests of single parents and their children. The group publishes *The Single Parent* magazine and other resource materials.

* Big Brothers, Big Sisters of America, 230 North 13th St., Philadelphia, PA 19107; (215) 567-7000; www.bbbsa.org. The national headquarters maintains lists of local agencies working with children from single-parent homes.

* Focus on the Family, Colorado Springs, CO 90993; (800) 232-6459; www.family.org. An evangelical ministry stressing traditional family values. They also publish a magazine called *Single Parent Family*, offering support and special encouragement for single parents.

* Social Services. Local offices are usually listed in the "County" section of your telephone directory. See such listings as "Public Health Services" and "Public Social Services Agency." The many services available include financial aid, food stamps, resources for emergency needs, adult education, day care, and housing.

Mom Me Time 5
Find a Counselor

In any mothering season, moms can find themselves needing the help a counselor can provide. The following is a list of steps to follow in locating a trustworthy and effective counselor:

1. Ask your friends and pastor for referrals. Watch for the same name coming up from different sources.
2. Check with several churches for referrals. Again watch for a recurring name. Larger churches in your community will probably have the most developed list.

3. Express your desire for a counselor who shares your faith and doctrinal beliefs.

4. Once you have identified a few counselors, call them and ask for a short interview on the phone. While interviewing them, ask the following:

* "Will you give me a list of references (pastors or professionals who recommend you)?"
* "Will you state your credentials and licensing?" Also ask for a disclosure form that details their counseling procedures and philosophy.
* "Do you have experience in (the specific issues you are dealing with)?"

These may include marriage difficulties, blended family issues, adultery, substance abuse, money problems, pornography, anxiety, physical abuse, eating disorders, low self-esteem, discipline problems, and so forth.

Keep in mind that counselors are not going to fix you. Their role is as facilitator. If you want change to take place, you need to accept responsibility for your own attitudes and behavior and have a willingness to change where indicated. Pursuing the help you need to become a healthy family may take a long-term commitment. Quick therapy is generally a Band-Aid over a gaping wound.[16]

Mom We Time

Get together and discuss your answers to the following questions:

1. How often do you ask for help?

    * Regularly
    * Only when I absolutely have to
    * H–h–h–help? I hardly ever use that word!

2. If you get help regularly, what kind of a difference does it make in your life? If you rarely ask for help, what keeps you from asking? How could you and your child or children benefit if you had help a little more often?

    _____

    _____

    _____

3. When it comes to the need for emotional help, does it surprise you that a high percentage of women suffer depression? Have you ever suspected you might be experiencing depression? As mothers who are connected to each other through this group and, perhaps, friendships, how can we support one another when one or more of us is dealing with depression? How can we make a difference in each other's mental outlook and in the realities we each live out day to day as mothers?

    _____

    _____

    _____

4. Sit quietly for a moment. Think of three to-dos that are priorities for you as you finish out today and look to tomorrow. Things as routine as stopping at the grocery store for food for dinner or as important as figuring out whether

your child may have a developmental problem. Write them down. Now take turns reading your to-dos to the others, if you feel comfortable doing so. As you read, have the group offer suggestions on how you might get help in carrying out this need. Can your children pitch in? Your husband? A neighbor? Or maybe someone in this group? Have a good time brainstorming together, thinking outside the box, and encouraging each other in finding and accepting help, in all its many forms.

For Further Reading

Books

Aldrich, Sandra P. *From One Single Mother to Another: Advice and Encouragement from Someone Who's Been There.*

Colopy, Elsa. *The Single Mom's Guide to Finding Joy in the Chaos: From One Who's Been There.*

Harley, Willard F., Jr. *His Needs, Her Needs: Building an Affair-Proof Marriage.*

Hart, Archibald, and Catherine Hart Weber. *Unveiling Depression in Women: A Practical Guide to Understanding and Overcoming Depression.*

Jarrell, Jane. *Secrets of a Mid-Life Mom.*

Kendall, Kathleen. *The Well-Ordered Home: Inviting Serenity into Your Home.*

Ladd, Karol, and Jane Jarrell. *The Frazzled Factor: Relief for Working Moms.*

Smallin, Donna. *Organizing Plain and Simple: A Ready Reference Guide with Hundreds of Solutions to Your Everyday Clutter Challenges.*

Walsh, Sheila. *Honestly* (a personal story about depression).

Wilson, Mimi, and Mary Beth Lagerborg. *Once-a-Month Cooking: A Proven System for Spending Less Time in the Kitchen and Enjoying Delicious, Homemade Meals Every Day.*

Websites

www.aacc.net. This website for the American Association of Christian Counselors includes resources and a directory to find a counselor.

www.babysittingcoop.com. This is a web resource by the authors of *Smart Mom's Babysitting Co-op Handbook.* It includes a downloadable starter kit.

www.cgin.org. The Cooperative Grocers' Information Network has lots of resources about food co-ops and an online guide, "How to Start a Co-op," that is beautifully illustrated and easy to read. Families can reap benefits from using a local co-op or from using these ideas on a smaller scale with other families.

www.depression.org. The website of the International Foundation for Research and Education on Depression; includes resources and fact sheets on depression.

www.depression-screening.org. The National Mental Health Association offers a confidential screening tool.

www.familysanitysavers.com. This site includes fun resources for lots of things to do with your family, including an eight-step starter guide for beginning a babysitting co-op.

www.flylady.net. This site offers strategies for home organization through a systematic approach to keeping up with chaos! The "Flylady" is a woman who once burned herself out trying to maintain a clean home. She encourages visitors with simple ideas and a witty sense of humor. Apart from discovering her system to maintaining order, site visitors can sign up for online mentoring and e-mail reminders. They can also find recipes, articles, and housekeeping tips from other members.

www.housecleaning-tips.com. This site provides articles and tips for organizing every room of the home. Visitors can access information about stain removal, carpet cleaning, and treating hardwood floors as well as guides to natural cleaning products and specific supplies that can help get tough jobs done around the house. You can also sign up for a weekly e-zine that covers these topics and others related to home repair and decorating.

www.nncc.org. This site for the National Network for Child Care has great resources for parents in general and guidelines for starting a healthy babysitting co-op.

www.organizedhome.com. This site provides guides to declutter and organize your home with articles, printable forms and planner, and access to an online community where you can find recipes, reader tips, and message boards. In addition to locating information about making your home function more efficiently, visitors can also participate in weekly goal-setting projects and keep track of their own progress in a personal online journal.

www.postpartum.com. Postpartum Support International offers resources for those with postpartum depression. Also offers information on local support groups.

Five

Perspective

I Want to Focus on What Matters

Fit today into the bigger picture of life.

MomSpeak

* I'm surprised I get so upset about unimportant things ... like a spilled drink.
* I need to know other moms experience the same frustrations and challenges that I do, and some encouragement that there is light at the end of the tunnel.
* An unexpected visitor drops by and I'm so embarrassed that everything is a mess, as if I never clean and straighten up.
* The hardest part of being a mother is not being able to control what another human being does.
* I need to be flexible. Trying to stick to my own agenda causes 80 percent of our family's hassles.
* Reality showed me I cannot be Supermom. The important thing is to leave a legacy and lead my children to God. The dishes can wait.

Anna stood at the kitchen sink, gazing out the window and daydreaming about the time when she wouldn't feel pulled in so many directions. Surely one day the house would be clean and she'd have some downtime. She eyed her scrapbooking box in the corner of the family room. Two years behind, and she wasn't doing much to change that these days. She couldn't think about scrapbooking when the house needed vacuuming, errands had to be run, laundry was always waiting, and Jose's mother, who lived downstairs, needed any attention she wasn't giving the kids.

Snapping back to reality, Anna remembered the water gushing from the faucet and began rinsing the breakfast dishes. Next, she wiped milk stains and sticky crumbs from the counter and swept the floor. Glancing into the family room, she saw her next task looming before her — cleaning the carpet littered with puzzle pieces, a plastic tea set, clothes, and crayons.

Just then she felt a tug on her jeans and looked down. "Mommy, can you read to me?" four-year-old Sofia pleaded, clutching her favorite book. Anna had read that book to Sofia hundreds of times in the past few weeks. "Not now, honey," Anna sighed. "Maybe later."

Sofia whined and then collapsed at her mother's feet, trapping Anna in place. "Sofia! Can't you see that Mommy is very busy today? I have to finish cleaning the kitchen, do the laundry, go to the store, take Nana to the doctor, and finish writing those thank-you notes for the presents we got when Sara was born! And now you've made a huge mess in the family room, and I have to clean that up too!"

"But Mommy—the kitchen *is* clean! And you always do laundry ... and the carpet doesn't look messy to me," Sofia pleaded.

"Not now, Sofia. Maybe later," Anna firmly repeated as she pried the child's arms from her legs and marched to the clothes dryer. She had only a few towels to fold, but Anna wasn't one to let them sit and get wrinkled.

The phone rang. It was her longtime girlfriend Christina. They'd been friends since grade school. After chatting for a few minutes and promising to get together soon so Christina could meet the baby, Anna went to check on napping Sara. Good, still asleep.

But where had Sofia taken herself? Peeking around the corner into her daughter's bedroom, Anna found Sofia sitting in her pint-sized rocking chair, holding a book and facing a row of attentive stuffed animals. They were arranged audience style and gave the appearance of applauding fans before a great talent.

Sofia began "reading" from her book, mimicking her mother's intonations. Then she snapped the book shut and announced to her eager audience, "I forgot. I don't have time to read today! I have too much to do!" Rising quickly from her rocker, she marched over to a doll baby, picked her up, and then plopped her down in a playpen. "No, I can't read to you now. Maybe later. And don't ask me again! Can't you see I am busy?"

Anna pulled herself back around the corner, leaned against the hall wall, and pondered the role-play she'd just observed. *Ouch! Is that really how Sofia sees me? From the mouth of a four-year-old ... I guess I sometimes forget what's important and lose my focus,* she realized.

What Every **MOM** Needs

Not now, maybe later. It's tough to hear that familiar mother-to-child answer and not feel a few pangs of guilt, isn't it? But this chapter isn't about guilt. It's about a larger struggle that we face day in and day out. The struggle to learn to cope with our busyness and find focus, or perspective. The struggle to balance the urgent and the important. The struggle to recognize our choices and make them with wisdom, so that we're less likely to feel guilty now or have regrets later.

What do we mean by "perspective"? Perspective is the ability to stand between yesterday and tomorrow and understand how and where today fits in. As the mothers of young children seeking to discover how our "todays" fit into our lifetime roles as women, we have to stand back and get a larger view of the whole of life. We have to identify some goals that transcend today and then remember what we're aiming toward.

Writer Annie Dillard hit upon this angle while staying in a friend's wilderness cabin. One day while attempting to chop some wood, she thought as she struggled, "What I did was less like splitting wood than chipping flints ... [until I discovered] you aim at the chopping block, not at the wood; then you split the wood, instead of chipping it. You cannot do the job cleanly unless you treat the wood as the transparent means to an end, aiming past it."[1]

Perspective means looking beyond the moment with a view toward the whole of life. And moms of preschoolers need perspective as they move through days in which the goal of a clean house can take precedence over tickle wars, and completing a to-do list may win out over laptime. Some moms are balancing not only children and to-dos, but a job or care for elderly parents as well. This kind of responsibility leaves us feeling sandwiched between urgent and competing needs, while still the home needs attention, and on and on.

Living with perspective is difficult at any stage or situation in life. The present is so demanding that it takes on meaning of its own, separate from its rightful place in the context of forever. And for the mother of preschoolers, several mothering myths worm their way into our thinking and distort our focus.

Mothering Myths and Reality

We've swallowed certain mothering myths as truths, unaware that it is falsehood that directs much of our thinking as well as our actions. As a result, we often forget why we're doing what we're doing and what really matters in the long run.

Following are four myths coupled with their corresponding realities, which could help you see where you might be misled in what motivates your mothering.

Myth 1: **If you control everything, life works.**
Reality: **You can't control everything. You have to go with the flow.**

We tend to believe that we should be in control at every moment, and that if we are, all the big and little things of life will run smoothly. John and Stasi Eldredge write, "We believe that in order to have the life we want, we must take matters into our own hands."[2]

Ha! That's like a dream ... and then we get up in the morning and face reality.

What Every **MOM** Needs

Exactly. The myth that we can make life work by being in control gives way to the reality that most of life is beyond our control. Trying to take charge of all events in life only leads to frustration and despair.

The reality is that life has a life of its own. Take children, for instance. Babies spit up on you just as you're ready to walk out the door. Toddlers wet their training pants three weeks after you thought they'd mastered toilet training. Kindergartners shyly hang back from their mothers on the first day of school, even though they've been impatiently checking off the days on a calendar for the past month.

Besides children, there is the everyday stuff of life that refuses our commands. Cars stall in traffic. Lines are long at the store. Three bills arrive on the same day. A filling breaks in a tooth. The milk spoils. A button pops off a shirt.

And then there is the unexpected. Your father has a heart attack. Your sister is in a bad car accident. Your husband needs knee surgery and is laid up for a month.

How do we handle the shattering of this myth of control? Apply a strong dose of practical action.

Relinquish Control

The Serenity Prayer, popular for overcoming many addictions, also speaks powerfully to the world of the mother of preschoolers. In those unforgettable words of Reinhold Neibuhr:

God, grant me the serenity to accept what cannot be changed,
Courage to change what should be changed,
And the wisdom to know the difference.

Moms who give over control to God report peace and rest. Deal with the myth that life can be controlled before you lose your perspective and sanity. Relinquish your attempts to control life, as this mom describes, "I'm up to my elbows in laundry, the phone is ringing, my toddler is spilling a box of cereal on the floor, the cat just puked on my freshly cleaned carpet, and as I bend down to clean it all up, I find a bill that slipped under the couch that needed to be paid yesterday. In stressful crazy days like that, usually my last thought is how God has planned my day. Since I've forgotten that, I freak out, stressing about how *I'm* going to have to figure it all out."

Respond Only to the Responsibility You've Been Given

So many of us borrow burdens from others. We decide we're responsible for a friend's happiness, for a child's health, for a husband's fulfillment.

Dr. Marianne Neifert, otherwise known as "Dr. Mom," admits candidly, "I can say: God didn't put all that stuff in my sack. When I looked inside, I saw my ambition, need for other people's approval, perfectionism. Those things were put there by me. That's why my sack was too heavy."[3]

Along these same lines, A. J. Russell, in his book *God Calling*, suggests that stress results from carrying two days' burdens in one day. His words echo those of Jesus: "Therefore do not worry about tomorrow, for tomorrow will worry about itself. Each day has enough trouble of its own" (Matthew 6:34).

Humor Helps

When the myth shatters that we can control life around us, humor helps.

Try this line: "God put me on earth to accomplish a certain number of things. Right now I am so far behind, I will never die." Learn to smile at your inability to control. Humor eases our hurts and frustrations as we admit our humanity!

Okay. Are you ready to shatter another myth?

Myth 2: **I should do it all right and all right now.**
Reality: **I can't do it all, but I can do what's important.**

Our expectations for ourselves and what we should be accomplishing are astronomically high and unrealistic. We've moved past the Supermom syndrome and climbed atop a pedestal of perfection. We assume that we should be able to do it all right and all right *now!*

Right? Wrong. "As challenges keep coming," Erma Bombeck once said, "mothers realize they can't possibly keep pace or they'll wind up comatose in the kitchen sink." We can fight against this second myth by taking deliberate steps to define and embrace what really matters in *this particular stage* of life.

Keep the Main Thing the Main Thing

In his book *First Things First*, Stephen Covey challenges his readers to define what really matters: "The main thing is to keep the main thing ... the main thing!" Covey stresses that we must intentionally commit ourselves to what is important, or we will be committing ourselves to what is unimportant.

For moms of preschoolers, perspective comes as we define what really matters in mothering.

What really matters to you as a mom? A clean home or a kind heart? Your children's habits or their values? Their appearance or their attitudes and actions? Of course, we might reply that *all* of these things are truly important. For example, children, and parents too, function better when their surroundings are neat and orderly. And we're all healthier when our home is clean. But when little Joey spills his milk just as you are preparing to leave for preschool, an understanding heart is more important than a clean table. In the same way, a child's habits certainly reflect his or her values, so forming good habits is important. But when we're faced with ten minutes before bed to clean a bedroom or to read and pray together, the latter is probably more valuable. You get the idea. When Maggie insists on wearing her princess costume to the grocery store *again*, we might choose to let this battle go and instead demand that she be kind to her brother as they ride next to each other in the car en route to the store. Perspective is restored when we define for ourselves just what it is that we're trying to accomplish as mothers.

Allocate the Investment of Your Time and Energy Based on "the Main Thing"

This myth of doing it all right and doing it all right *now* leads us to pay too much attention to the niggling little details of life. When we define for ourselves what really matters, we can then use such a definition as a measuring stick of our activities. Where are we spending our energies?

One mom said, "I find myself frustrated with my little boy because he demands too much of my attention while I'm trying to get dinner together or fold laundry or whatever. So I try to get him involved in other activities, but he feels that he is being snubbed, so he decides to bring some sand in from outside or climb up and pound on the computer. Before I know it, I'm in a power struggle with him, all because I seem to think that having dinner ready fifteen minutes earlier is more important than sitting with him during a time of day when he is less able to control his impulses. It is times like these that I need to step back and remind myself of what the priorities are."

Admittedly, there are times when it's tough to know whether an issue falls under "the main thing."

Another mom revealed, "Just when I think it's okay to go through the day in sweats, wear only lipstick or no makeup, and let the house look less than perfect while I spend time nurturing and playing with my children (who won't be children forever) … and that it's okay not to look perfect (pre-pregnant weight, hair washed and styled, up-to-date clothes), my husband returns home from work with a comment about the house being a mess or dinner not being on the table or 'What did you do all day and what's wrong with your hair?' Ouch!"

Such a comment is a red flag reminder to communicate and agree upon values with your husband. Still, ticklish days do reveal choices about what matters most. Should you go on the preschool field trip or go to a coffee shop with a friend? In such moments, ask yourself: What need is more pressing right now? What will matter in five years? What should I do that only *I* can do? or, What would happen if I ignored this issue? Such questions provide the parameters we need to keep our focus.

Here's a third mothering myth. See if you can relate.

Myth 3: **The best way to make it through mothering is to grin and bear it until it gets better.**

Reality: **Enjoy today. Make the most of life's irretrievable moments … now.**

How much of what is good about mothering do we miss because our focus is simply on getting through it? Sure, we all see truth in the face of well-intentioned advice from kindly grandmothers in grocery stores who tell us (as we wrestle with three cranky kids in the checkout line), "These are the best days of your life! Enjoy them because they pass so quickly!"

"*This* day couldn't pass quickly enough," we mutter under our breath.

But these women do have a point. One that comes with the wisdom of their years. The stage of mothering young children is a *stage*. It only *feels* like an era! And it will pass. It will not last forever. It will end one day.

When we accept the myth that the best we can do is to simply "grin and bear it," we miss out on what mothering can mean. While we're wishing ourselves into the next season, we miss the good stuff that's happening now. This myth is shattered when we deliberately determine to make the most of life's irretrievable moments.

Here's how:

Live in the Present

How quickly we push past today to reach tomorrow!

*First I was dying to finish high school
and start college.
And then I was dying to finish
college and start working.
And then I was dying to marry
and have children.
And then I was dying for my children
to grow old enough for school
so I could return to work.*

What Every **MOM** Needs

And then I was dying to retire.
And now, I am
dying . . .
And suddenly I realize I forgot to live.

—Anonymous

Today you are indispensably valuable in the life of someone else!

A hundred years from now ... it will not matter what my bank account was, the sort of house I lived in, or the kind of car I drove ... but the world may be different because I was important in the life of a child.

—Anonymous

This week you have the opportunity to get on the floor and build block towers. This is the season when you are invited to read, to play, to imagine, to dream! Your lap is the "favoriteest place to be." Your smile is more valuable than money. Your words mean more than those on the television, in a magazine, or in a classroom. Savor the moments of this season that will never come around again.

We tend to keep waiting for life to get better when, really, it just gets different. If the grass looks greener on the other side of your fence, it may be because you're not investing your time and energy in your own grass. Live in the present.

Enjoy the Little Things

Treasure each moment. Like precious stones, they are yours to touch, appreciate, and store in your heart to ponder and relive.

For life is short, the years rush past.
A little boy grows up so fast.
No longer is he at your side,
His precious secrets to confide.
The picture books are put away.
There are no more games to play.
No goodnight kiss, no prayers to hear—
That all belongs to yesteryear.
My hands once busy now lie still.
The days are long and hard to fill.
I wish I might go back and do
The little things you asked me to.

—Anonymous

One last mothering myth tends to rob us of our mothering perspective.

Myth 4: **Mothering is serious business, and the lives of your children are at stake at every moment.**

Reality: **Lighten up. Children are resilient. Handle them with honesty and humor.**

Fear obscures perspective. Focusing on the worst-case scenario, the unimaginable horror of what even remotely might lie ahead, our fears leap out of all proportion and blur our vision of reality.

And our fears multiply: "If Grandma feeds your baby a food or dairy product before the doctor has instructed it, your child may suffer allergies for the rest of her life." "If you let your child cry for even a few minutes, you will endanger the bonding process, and studies show that a disruption in bonding is often the cause of criminal behavior later in life."

We have so much information available to us today, and we hear stories on the news about one-in-a-million kidnappings, child accidents, unusual diseases, and injuries. Yes, it *could* happen to my child. We should take all reasonable precautions. But living in constant fear of all the "what-ifs" takes a lot out of the day-to-day joy we should be experiencing with our kids. While mothering is crucial and good mothering even more valuable, falling victim to the fear of ruining our children with a single mistake is unrealistic. Fight off this myth by recognizing that children are resilient, and most children will stay alive and well to become healthy adults.

Honor Your Children with Honesty

When you make a mistake, learn to forgive yourself and let go of your failure. Refuse to pack up your guilt and carry it with you. Say you're sorry and move on. When your child asks a question, tell her the truth. Children do not expect their mothers to be perfect—unless we have taught them to expect perfection. They will respond with respect when inadequacies are shared appropriately.

Handle Your Children with Humor

In his book *The Strong Family*, Chuck Swindoll warns us to avoid a pessimistic outlook. "Call me crazy if you like (you won't be the first), but I am more convinced than ever that attitudes shape just about everything we do. Not facts, not a group of so-called authorities. Not some big, thick book spelling the demise of civilization ... but attitudes."[4]

Lighten up and laugh at yourself. Children most often respond to a light touch, not a heavy hand. Teach them to laugh at themselves as well. Make "Oops!" the password of your home. Find something extra in the ordinary to celebrate. Take mothering just a little bit less seriously and watch how you blossom—and your children along with you!

Four myths of mothering. If we believe what they stand for, we're sure to lose our focus. But when we replace them with reality, perspective returns.

A Perspective of Choice

One of the most challenging aspects of mothering is the challenge of choices. How do I know if I can/should go through delivery without medication? Should I go back to work after the baby is born? Should I try and work at home? What philosophy of discipline will work best for my child? How do I choose a school or day care program? And what about me? How and when should I take time for myself? What really matters in the long run?

Perspective offers the wisdom needed to make such choices on a daily basis. Perspective is fitting today in between yesterday and tomorrow. It's understanding that today has value as it grows out of yesterday and as it shapes tomorrow. Perspective gives mothers of preschoolers the ability to endure the mundane tasks and demands of today because that attention prepares our children for the future.

Various descriptions have been used to explain the choice-making dilemma faced by mothers.

What Are Your Priorities?

Perspective for choice making is said to be simplified when you identify your priorities. But the process may not be as clear or simple as it sounds. For one thing, setting priorities takes time, usually time away from the distractions of the urgent. Time to fit today between yesterday and tomorrow. Time to think back and look forward. And time to wrestle with the consequences of your choices.

For instance, if your priority is to do what you can to bring up a healthy, happy, well-adjusted child, and you believe that the influence you have on your child as her mother is crucial to her development, you'll stop working outside or inside the home, right? Maybe ... but perhaps your husband has lost his job, or is transitioning to another career and earning less, or has left you, or died. Your children need to have their financial needs met. Or maybe you honestly feel you are a better, healthier mom for your kids if you are living out another side of yourself through some employment. Maybe you feel a clear calling from God to work at something alongside your mothering. The priority is clear, but the choices leave much room for uncertainty.

Your husband may also be a priority. He wants you to spend more time alone with him. But your baby is sick and crying for you. How do you meet both needs? Which one gets top priority? Whose need do you put first?

You may recognize a priority for giving yourself a break and an opportunity for growth now and then in order to be fresh and effective as a mom. But what do you do when your toddler comes down with a cold the night of your first seminar, or when your husband comes home tired from a long day and looks forward to having you home but you're supposed to go out to a meeting?

There are times when an assignment of priorities is both easy and helpful. But there are many other moments when the picture is not so clear, and the pieces keep shifting like the pattern in a kaleidoscope, which changes as you slowly rotate it in the light. There is no single clear priority all the time, or rigid, predetermined first-, second-, and third-place priority rankings which lead to the right choices.

What Is This Balancing Act?

Another view of perspective for choice making is the balancing act. Choices are made on the basis of how good we are at juggling.

Like a circus act, a mom takes one plate and spins it on a stick above her head. No problem. But then another plate is added, so she must spin both plates. A bit later, here comes another and then another, until she is spinning four and then five plates above her head. As if this were not enough, some new responsibility hits her around one leg, and she finds she must stand with all her weight on only one foot. Looking down, she realizes that her once-secure footing has been replaced by a thin wire suspended high above the ground. With perspiration beading her brow, she fights for balance while keeping all the plates in motion. Because, of course, she must.

Elizabeth Phillips Runkle shares her opinion on this balancing act from the view of a working woman. Responding to a Ph.D. on a television talk show, expounding on how to achieve total balance in her life and the world around her, Runkle writes,

> Balance? I could tell that woman on the TV a few things about balance.
>
> Balance is keeping the mom-mobile on the highway while simultaneously signing the homework paper

that was due last week, tying the five-year-old's shoes, keeping him from hitting his sister, and getting the whole carload to school only five minutes after the last bell and still arriving at work on time.

Balance is following the liturgy and looking prayerful while gently suspending the littlest one by the scruff of the neck and whispering in his ear, "We're in church! Cut out the anatomical sounds!"

Balance is holding a kid on each hip and a two-hundred-fifty pound dog on a leash while watching the clouds open up with a vengeance.

Balance is climbing to the mountaintop at work all day and digging through the mound of laundry at night.[5]

Life can't be kept neatly in balance. As soon as you decide that every child will only participate in one "outside" activity, your progeny are selected for children's chorale and make it to the finals of the state swim meet. We need something more than a balancing act to direct our perspective regarding choice making.

Seasonal Perspective

Perhaps the most sensible approach to understanding perspective for choice making is the seasonal perspective. In this view, life is broken down into various seasons, each characterized by its own priorities and its own criteria for choice making. Looking at the *whole* of life with all its seasons enables us to gain perspective within each season.

The Bible describes this seasonal perspective in the book of Ecclesiastes:

There is a time for everything,
and a season for every activity under heaven:
a time to be born and a time to die,
a time to plant and a time to uproot,
a time to kill and a time to heal,
a time to tear down and a time to build,
a time to weep and a time to laugh,
a time to mourn and a time to dance,
a time to scatter stones and a time to gather them,
a time to embrace and a time to refrain,
a time to search and a time to give up,
a time to keep and a time to throw away,
a time to tear and a time to mend,
a time to be silent and a time to speak,
a time to love and a time to hate,
a time for war and a time for peace.

—Ecclesiastes 3:1–8

A time to mother tiny children and a time to mother older ones. A time to hold babies and a time to let them go. A time to focus on our children and a time to give attention to ourselves and our dreams. As one mother of a preschooler put it:

I love autumn. It is my favorite time of year, but I felt frustrated that it is such a brief season until I realized that its beauty is so poignant because it is framed by summer and winter. As a mother of a preschooler, I have to remind myself that each stage of life has its immense wonder, yet they all must move on. It is only in the moving on that we can fully appreciate what has passed.

What Every **MOM** Needs

In her book *A Season at Home*, Debbie Barr writes about making choices with this seasonal perspective, which she describes as "sequencing," a process that allows women to concentrate on each of life's major tasks at the proper time.

> Sequencing means narrowing the scope of our pursuits so as to give priority to children when they are young. Then, as the seasons of life unfold, we expand into other pursuits gradually, according to the guidance of God. Sequencing ... allows us to say "I love you" to our children in the most convincing way possible: by being there during the season of their lives when they need the most nurture and physical care. As our children's seasons change, we move into new seasons as well.[6]

Such an understanding of the whole of life helps us to pay closer attention to where we are. We see the importance of choosing to invest in our children now—the season of their greatest need for us—knowing that other seasons will come later. "Not now, maybe later" points its finger, reminding us that we are not sacrificing ourselves forever. And reminding us that investment of time in our children now will pay dividends later as they become more independent, allowing us freedom to pursue other interests.

Mother-poet Joy Jacobs expresses her own commitment to sequencing in her poem "Mysteries of Motherhood":

> *Yesterday I found a fingernail in the toaster,*
> *Today the dryer yields just seven socks.*
> *Ah, mysteries of life:*

Whence fingernails?
Where socks?
Where are the mates?
And why not six or eight?
I long to search for Holy Grails
Or even joust at windmills....
Instead, I rewash glasses
Left less than spot-free
By eager childish hands
And hang sheets out on windy days
And never do catch sight
of one brave armored knight.
But when a little boy thanks God at night
For "the best mommy in the world"—
Strange windmills lose their charm
And I'm content
To fetch a grail of water
Before he goes to sleep.
Quixote, wait another year!
I still am needed here.[7]

Keeping Things in Perspective

Perspective is the ability to stand between yesterday and tomorrow and understand how today fits and what matters most. How very much moms of preschoolers need perspective! We need to know that we're making a difference when we put a bit of ourselves on the shelf for a while. When we drop everything to hold our babies while they are sick, disregard the clutter to read to our toddlers, turn down a promotion at work, or just be present as a "home base" from which our

What Every **MOM** Needs

little ones can go out to explore — we need to know that we've chosen well.

Max Lucado captures our need for perspective as he writes about a group of climbers scaling a tall mountain while keeping their snow-capped goal in sight:

> On clear days the crested point reigned as king on the horizon. Its white tip jutted into the blue sky inviting admiration and offering inspiration.
>
> On days like this the hikers made the greatest progress. The peak stood above them like a compelling goal. Eyes were called upward. The walk was brisk. The cooperation was unselfish....
>
> Yet on some days the peak of the mountain was hidden from view. The cloud covering would eclipse the crisp blueness with a drab, gray ceiling and block the vision of the mountaintop. On these days the climb became arduous. Eyes were downward and thoughts inward. The goal was forgotten. Tempers were short. Weariness was an uninvited companion. Complaints stung like thorns on the trail.
>
> We're like that, aren't we? As long as we can see our dream, as long as our goal is within eyesight, there is no mountain we can't climb or summit we can't scale. But take away our vision, block our view of the trail's end, and the result is as discouraging as the journey.[8]

Yes! As they experience the inner pulls and tugs of mothering little-bitty ones, moms need to remember the bigger picture.

IF YOU GIVE A MOM A MUFFIN
by Kathy Fictorie

If you give a mom a muffin,
She'll want a cup of coffee to go with it.
She'll pour herself some.
The coffee will get spilled by her three-year-old.
She'll wipe it up.
Wiping the floor, she will find some dirty socks.
She'll remember she has to do some laundry.
When she puts the laundry in the washer,
She'll trip over some snow boots and bump into the freezer.
Bumping into the freezer will remind her she has to plan
*   supper for tonight.*
She will get out a pound of hamburger.
She'll look for her cookbook. (101 Things to Make with a
*   Pound of Hamburger.)*
The cookbook is sitting under a pile of mail.
She will see the phone bill which is due tomorrow.
She will look for her checkbook.
The checkbook is in her purse that is being dumped out by her
*   two-year-old.*
She'll smell something funny.
She'll change the two-year-old.
While she is changing the two-year-old the phone will ring.
*   (Of course!)*
Her five-year-old will answer it and hang up.
She remembers that she wants to phone a friend to come for
*   coffee on Friday.*
Thinking of coffee will remind her that she was going to have
*   a cup.*

She will pour herself some.
And chances are,
If she has a cup of coffee,
Her kids will have eaten the muffin that went with it.[9]

Here's an idea to help you appreciate your children, right where they are. Copy this poem on a piece of paper and put it on your refrigerator, along with your child's handprint:

HANDPRINT
Anonymous

Sometimes you get discouraged
Because I am so small
And always leave my fingerprints
On furniture and walls.
But every day I'm growing up
And soon I'll be so tall,
That all those little handprints
Will be hard to recall.
So here's a special handprint
Just so that you can say
This is how my fingers looked
When I placed them here today.

Mom Me Time

Mom Me Time 1
Root Out Myth from Reality

Determine some of your own mothering myths and realities by answering these questions:

1. What are some of the myths about mothering that echo in your mind like a broken record? (Example: "If it's worth doing, it's worth doing well.") Which ones are valuable to keep? Which are not?

2. What are your greatest fears or worries as a mother?

3. What are your greatest frustrations?

4. Which answers from the last two questions can you control?

5. Which are beyond your control?

What Every **MOM** Needs

6. How will you intentionally "let go" of what you can't control?

7. What do you want most for your child? Are your goals apparent?

8. What are you doing to make progress toward these goals?

9. What are your priorities in this season of life?

10. How are they different from your life priorities before you had children?

11. What different priorities will you have when all your kids are in school? When all of them have left home?

12. What do you like best about this season of life? What do you like least? Is there anything you could do to increase time for what you enjoy and decrease time spent on what you don't like?

_____

_____

_____

13. What advice about this season would you offer to a new mother?

_____

_____

_____

14. How do you follow that advice?

_____

_____

Mom Me Time 2
Perfectionism and Perspective

Are you a perfectionist? Your perfectionism could be making it difficult for you to keep perspective in your mothering and even in life in general. Use this season of mothering young children to work at moving away from perfectionism. With conscious effort you can choose to devote your energy to what matters most to you now and in the long term.

Take the following test, adapted for moms. Evaluate yourself honestly and check those that describe you most accurately.

PERFECTIONIST MOM VERSUS
HEALTHY PERSPECTIVIST MOM

Perfectionist	Healthy Perspectivist
❏ I set standards for a clean home, my marriage, my own work life, or my children's behavior that are beyond reach and reason.	❏ I have high standards for cleanliness, a healthy marriage, my personal pursuits, and my children's behavior, but I keep a sense of humor, knowing my joy in life isn't dependent on these standards being met.
❏ I'm never honestly satisfied with my home, family life, and personal pursuits unless they appear pretty close to perfection.	❏ I enjoy the *process* of creating and maintaining a home, experiencing family life, and pursuing personal dreams as well as the *outcome*.
❏ A dirty house or lack of money to decorate makes me into a crazy woman. When family life isn't fun and fulfilling, my disillusionment makes me depressed. When my child displays traits I don't like, I panic.	❏ A dirty house and shabby furniture bug me, but I try to take it in stride, knowing things will change in time. When family life seems bogged down in diapers and illness and squabbling, I eat some chocolate and realize how much these people mean to me. When my child displays traits I don't like, I marvel that he really is his own person.

❏ If I look deeply, I must admit that I'm trying to meet an ideal that exists somewhere out there for what a family home should look like, how my kids should look and act, and what kind of appearance and achievement I should reach as a woman and mom. Anything less and I'd be considered a failure.	❏ I read the magazines and I know the unwritten code of what it means to be a mom who looks good and handles life well. These are nice images and they inspire me, but I also know what it means to live a real life and make choices that may look less than ideal on the outside. I'm okay with bucking the tide pretty regularly.
❏ I've made some mistakess as a mom that I consider to be fairly significant. I can't shake the feeling that I'm a bad, unfit mother.	❏ Yes, I've made my share of mistakes already as a mom. I know I survived my own mom's mistakes, and I'm just focusing on learning from my mistakes and carrying on.
❏ I admit that I'm very defensive when criticized. After all, I've worked incredibly hard at my mothering and my life as a woman. I'm insulted that someone would think there is a better way to do it than my way.	❏ I can always use help. I don't necessarily like to be criticized, but I will always take a look at another way of doing things. After all, much of what I do well I've learned from others.

What Every **MOM** Needs

Now tally your results. Are you more of a perfectionist or a "perspectivist"? If you tend toward perfectionism, realize that these tendencies may be hurting you more than helping you. Check out the book *Perfectionism: What's Bad about Being Too Good?* by Miriam Aderholdt and Jan Goldberg, or another resource you may find on moving away from perfectionism. Remember, perfectionism and the pursuit of excellence are not the same thing. Perfectionists often get sidetracked from excellence in their pursuit of "perfection"!

Mom Me Time 3

Keeping Perspective When Caring for Both Children and Aging Parents

Do you find yourself pressed on both sides, with children to care for as well as a parent who is aging, ill, or in need of your assistance regularly? Yes, many of us moms today are caught in the middle of this "sandwich" of caregiving. Keeping perspective when we feel tired and stretched to the max can be difficult.

Jane Jarrell, in her book *Secrets of a Mid-Life Mom*, writes, "Mid-life moms struggling with responsibilities to parents, husbands, and children often feel a nagging sense that nothing is being done right. We can feel as if our hearts are being torn in two — our children on one side, our parents on the other, in a seemingly endless tug-of-war. The emotions involved are enormous: gratitude to those who were always there to help us; frustration at the loss of what was; resentment and anger at the lack of control; compassion for the sorrows and pains of others; and sometimes overwhelming personal stress."[10]

Jarrell encourages moms to pay attention to important priorities while honoring and caring for your parent:

* Protect your marriage.
* Protect your children.
* Protect your emotional, physical, and spiritual self.
* Protect your job, if you have one and must keep it for financial or personal reasons.

How are you doing in holding to these priorities? Is there one you have let slide and need to spend time and attention restoring?

Mom Me Time 4
Keeping Perspective, Both as a Mom and a World Citizen

In her book *The Myth of the Perfect Mother*, Carla Barnhill devotes a chapter to the "social disconnect" that mothers experience. "We moms often joke that we have no idea what's going on in the 'real world' because we haven't read a newspaper or stayed awake for an entire newscast since our children arrived.... Motherhood ... brings with it a kind of social disconnect that has a deep impact on the emotional and spiritual lives of women."

Barnhill goes on to encourage mothers to stay informed as they are able and to find manageable ways to continue to give to the world in the areas they feel especially called or gifted. "I truly believe that when God gives us both a family and a vision for kingdom work, God will help us find a way to keep both in balance and to successfully meet the needs of our children in the midst of our efforts at blessing the world."[11]

Have you, as a mom, been able to stay in touch with the world and particular ways you can give to the world? If not, how could you begin taking some small steps in that direction?

_____

_____

_____

Mom Me Time 5
Remember God's Perspective

In keeping perspective, it's important to remember God's role in our lives. According to the Bible, he has specific good in store for each of us. "'For I know the plans I have for you,' declares the LORD, 'plans to prosper you and not to harm you, plans to give you hope and a future'" (Jeremiah 29:11).

List one area where you have lost perspective lately. What are you stressed about? What frustration are you dealing with?

_____

_____

_____

Now listen for a few moments to what God may be saying to you through his words above, then record his answer below.

_____

_____

_____

Mom We Time

Get together with other moms and discuss your answers to these questions:

1. We've said, "Moms of preschoolers need perspective as they move through days in which the goal of a clean house can take precedence over tickle wars, and completing a to-do list may win out over laptime." On a continuum, where would you say you fall right now on keeping perspective? Are you more focused on cleaning and to-dos or tickle wars and laptime? What is your motivation for your focus?

1	2	3	4	5	6	7	8	9	10
Clean house, to-do list					and		Tickle wars and laptime		

2. Which mothering myth listed in this chapter is most easy for you to buy into:

   ❏ If you control everything, life works.
   ❏ I should do it all right and all right now.
   ❏ The best way to make it through mothering is to grin and bear it until it gets better.
   ❏ Mothering is serious business, and the lives of my children are at stake every moment.

   Share honestly with each other, knowing that we all buy into all of these myths at one time or another in our motherhood.

3. How are *you* losing out by buying into this myth? How is your family losing out when you buy into this myth? Can

you think of one concrete thing you could do to move away from this myth?

4. What is it that most helps you keep an eye on the "bigger picture" of your role as a mother? What have you found helps you to keep a good balance between "doing" the necessary things in your life and "being" in relationship with your kids?

For Further Reading

Aderholdt, Miriam, and Jan Goldberg. *Perfectionism: What's Bad about Being Too Good?*

Barnhill, Carla. *The Myth of the Perfect Mother: Rethinking the Spirituality of Women.*

Barnhill, Julie Ann. *She's Gonna Blow! Real Help for Moms Dealing with Anger.*

Covey, Steven. *Seven Habits of Highly Effective People: Powerful Lessons in Personal Change.*

Edwards, Judith. *Supermom Has Left the Building: Being a Proverbs 31 Woman in a Twenty-first-Century World.*

Kuykendall, Carol. *Five-Star Families: Moving Yours from Good to Great.*

Ladd, Karol, and Jane Jarrell. *The Frazzled Factor: Relief for Working Moms*.

Lindbergh, Anne Morrow. *Gift from the Sea*.

MacDonald, Gordon. *Ordering Your Private World*.

Morgan, Elisa, and Carol Kuykendall. *Real Moms: Exploding the Myths of Motherhood*.

Schaeffer, Edith. *What Is a Family?*

Wilson, Deena Lee. *A Mom's Legacy: Five Simple Ways to Say Yes to What Counts Forever*.

Six

Hope

I Want to Find Deeper Meaning in Life

Hope is a relationship between God and me.
God knows me, stays with me, cares about my feelings,
and helps me be the best mother I can be.

MomSpeak

* I've just had my first baby. The process of pregnancy and childbirth, and now this baby—wow. I keep thinking, *There must be a God.* I can't stop kissing my baby. I think I want to know this God who gave me such an incredible gift. But I'm not sure what to do.

* I've never experienced such emotional highs and lows as I have in being a mother. Total euphoria and then what feels like close to a mental breakdown. I can't shake the feeling that motherhood is supposed to point me to something bigger. Maybe some*one* bigger.

* I've been religious all my life. It's always been a large part of what I do and who I am. But since I've become a mom, I've said things to God I never have before: "God, I *need* you. I need *help. Please* show me what to do and help me get through this. Take care of my kids for me—I can't seem to get it right as a mother!"

* I see now that my real need has always been for God. Motherhood is too hard to go it alone. I was so overwhelmed with the birth of my second son that I didn't think I'd make it. I remember sitting on the stairs of our townhouse, holding my baby while the toddler was "somewhere," and I cried out that I just couldn't do it anymore. Shortly after that, I asked Jesus to take hold of my life. Now he does it and I help.

* This is one thing I've learned: If you want to know Jesus, become a mom. You get a taste of the kind of love he feels. And you get a taste of what it means to give up your life for someone else. I think I can see Jesus a little more clearly every day I spend as a mom.

Kylah sneaked away as the voice of Albert Brooks captured her kids, and Marlin, Dory, and Nemo began flitting across the TV screen. Maybe, just maybe she wouldn't be noticed for fifteen or twenty minutes. Kylah slipped into the bathroom, closed the door ever so quietly, and locked it. She dug into the top of the medicine cabinet for matches and lit a scented candle. *Ahhhhh. Aromatherapy. Come on baby, do your thing. If there's something I need today, it's some therapy!* She sank down onto the lid of the toilet and took a deep breath. Kylah *really* needed a break. And an escape to her tiny bathroom felt like a pathetic substitute for the kind of break she really needed.

She'd been up since five in the morning with Marcus and Briana. Marcus had been waking early these days. Something about his blanket tickling him. Briana had ears like radar, and she always began wailing about five minutes after Marcus got out of bed. The day began with Marcus having a major fit because she peeled his banana too far, a dishwasher full of dirty dishes because she'd forgotten to start it the night before, and a potty accident on the carpet before it was even 8 a.m. They had all gone to the grocery store, with Marcus pulling his usual "gimmes," and then to the park, where Briana shrieked every time Kylah tried to take her out of the swing to go check on Marcus. Now they were home, fed, and up from ten-minute naps after being awakened by a jackhammer working on the asphalt across the street. She knew the kids would really be cranky by dinnertime.

Life in general was feeling like just too much. Being a mom to her kids, keeping the house clean and running, finding time for her husband, staying in touch with Mom and Dad and the in-laws, keeping up with her freelance graphics work at home, and trying to squeeze pick-me-ups with friends and family in between all of it so that she could feel like she had a life. Is this all there would ever be?

Yes, she loved her kids with a fierceness she couldn't even describe. She wouldn't give up being a mom for anything, and she had a lot more to like about her life, she knew. But she couldn't escape this feeling that it still just wasn't enough.

Breathe, relax, she told herself. The voices of Nemo and Marlin broke into her reverie: "Come back! Nemo, you come back here right now!" *Funny, someday I won't be enough for my kids. They'll start moving away from me into that big ocean out there. I know my heart will want to scream, "Come back here right now!" But these days, it's me wanting to get away, to find some adventure that will satisfy. I don't want my kids to grow up. But sometimes I don't know if I can handle them being little and so needy. There has to be more than my kids and this life as I know it, great as it is. Something deeper. Something that fills me up and brings light to what I know now and what I'm going to live through in the future. Some kind of hope that lasts . . .*

"Mommy, come back! You come back here right now! Come watch Nemo with us! And Bri smells stinky! Mommy?"

Hopeless Situations

Have you ever felt like this mother? Your best friend is moving away, far away, and you wonder how you'll make it without her. Your mother has cancer and needs you, but you have a baby who also needs you. Your husband just lost his job, and your job isn't going to pay all the bills. You're pregnant again and wonder in your heart if you can really afford . . . love . . . or cope with another child. Your marriage

What Every **MOM** Needs

is stale and old. Your neighborhood is full of crime — it's not safe to walk to the store anymore. Your house is a mess. Not only is there stuff everywhere, but the kitchen needs remodeling, the bathtub drain is clogged, and the carpet is covered with stains. Your children aren't what you had in mind. One has been diagnosed with a disorder you don't understand, and the other could teach Dr. Phil a thing or two about the meaning of a strong will.

You wouldn't trade your kids for anything, but a part of you can't shake this funk you're in. Life isn't turning out the way you expected, and it feels really crummy knowing there isn't a thing you can do about it.

Misplaced Hope

You feel a spark of hope in the thought of a getaway. If you could just get away from the walls of home and breathe some fresh air, see some new sights ... *A vacation! That's what I need!* So you make a plan, pack up husband and kids and two bags full of toys to keep them entertained in a cramped car, drive all night and half the next day, and check into a hotel exhausted. The room doesn't have that lovely mountain view promised in the brochure. It looks out over the parking lot. The kids are raring to go, and you want to sleep. It rains for three days. Your youngest gets sick. And the sun comes out the day you leave.

Then you try exercise. It's super being out of the house, moving your muscles. You feel refreshed and renewed when you return home. But your mood evaporates quickly when you face the dog mess on the carpet and the trash your toddler has gotten into and strewn all over the house.

Next you think of people. Surely if you could just rev up your marriage a little and reconnect, you would find that your husband would fill up that emptiness that's been nagging at you. After all, it's *people* we really can't live without. Between errands and during precious naptime, you squeeze in a trial run on a new recipe, set a romantic table, and put the kids to bed early so you can be alone with him. But he wants to watch the game on TV. Or you call a good friend, arrange for a baby-sitter, and set a date for lunch. But she gets the flu. And you end up taking her kids as well as yours so she can sleep.

Okay. Maybe it's time to get spiritual. You consider checking out a church somewhere nearby. But as you look through the phone book you think again. This stuff works for some people, but it's never been your thing. God, if there is one, is everywhere, so why the need for church? Why should you make the effort to get dressed and take the kids out just to go through the motions of religion? Or maybe you are a Christian. You've been attending church for years and you believe the Bible, but God just doesn't seem present in these busy, emotion-packed days of your life with young children.

Now you're back where you started. Still feeling this yearning that has no answer. Maybe there will never be any kind of light to brighten up all these trying days, or give you strength to watch your children grow up and away, or calm you as you grow old and face aging and death. Maybe it's just you, and aromatherapy is about all you can count on.

No, it's not good enough, you decide. I'm the mom. I'm the adult. I'm leading the way for my kids. There has to be a better way ...

What Every **MOM** Needs

This is the toughest stuff of life. It's the place we all come to eventually, if we slow down long enough to really think, feel, and experience it. The answers we've tried don't work. There must be something more, we realize. And there is.

It's a person. We were right, in a way, when we turned to the people in our life. But only one person can be all we need. That person is Jesus. Jesus is God, and he lived on this earth and experienced life as a human being, with all its exhilaration, all its daily tedium, and all its gut-wrenching struggle. He loved children. And he knew days without sleep, years without much money, seasons of caring for sick and needy people, and times of being unappreciated. Indeed, he shares the heart of a mother. And he loved women. In a day when women were treated as second class, he lived out his care and his esteem for women by reaching out to them and including them in his ministry. Jesus put more value in relationships than anything else.

That's why he died for you and me. You probably know the story. He was unjustly accused and put on a cross to die. He could have walked away, or simply disappeared and gone back to heaven. But he stayed and experienced an excruciating death. It was excruciating physically because he was carrying the weight of our sin on himself. That religious-sounding word—*sin*—is important for us moms. We try hard and we may have a lot going for us, but each of us sins; sin is a part of who we are. It's a part of every human being who lives. Sin is the motivation inside us to manage life on our own rather than in relationship with God. Sin is insisting *we* know what is best. The thing about sin is that it puts a kind of veil — a barrier — between God and us. It keeps us out of touch with God's strength, his power, his quiet peace. It keeps us out of the one relationship that will really fill the empty place.

Jesus came to change that. His death and his resurrection ripped away that veil. Now we can come to God and, through relationship with him, have daily companionship, help, peace, and hope as we walk toward the future as mothers, as women.

Just Another Religion?

Is Christianity just another religion? One among many in that grab bag of religions out there? Jesus offers us something very different from what any other world religion can offer. Listen to this story about C. S. Lewis, the creator of Narnia:

> During a British conference on comparative religions, experts from around the world debated what, if any, belief was unique to the Christian faith. They began eliminating possibilities. Incarnation? Other religions had different versions of gods appearing in human form. Resurrection? Again, other religions had accounts of return from death. The debate went on for some time until C. S. Lewis wandered into the room. "What's the rumpus about?" he asked, and heard in reply that his colleagues were discussing Christianity's unique contribution among world religions. Lewis responded, "Oh, that's easy. It's grace."
>
> After some discussion, the conferees had to agree. The notion of God's love coming to us free of charge,

What Every **MOM** Needs

no strings attached, seems to go against every instinct of humanity. The Buddhist eight-fold path, the Hindu doctrine of Karma, the Jewish covenant, and Muslim code of law—each of these offers a way to earn approval. Only Christianity dares to make God's love unconditional.[1]

We don't have to earn it. We don't have to check off requirements, like a to-do list. Instead of spending our life striving, we can spend it in relationship with a God who loves us, not one who is telling us to find the help inside ourselves or prove we love him by going through prescribed motions.

Invite Jesus into your life. He doesn't force himself on anyone. So tell him you want his life to live in you. Tell him you need his forgiveness and you want that veil removed between God and you. You may not be sure you believe it all, but if even a part of you does, give it a try. Jesus will help you with your unbelief.

Read this simple prayer and make it your own.

Jesus, I'm empty. I want to know you and have you fill this emptiness. I've tried. I can't. I need your help. I believe you died on the cross for my sins. Please forgive me. Please come into my life and begin a relationship with me. Amen.

Been There, Done That

This may be familiar talk to you. Have you been a Christian for a while? Have you heard the Jesus stories umpteen times? Is church a regular part of your life? Maybe you have gone through the motions for years, but it's been just that—motions but not much heart involvement. Have you been living day to day with Jesus as your friend, your confidant, your guide, your giver of light and hope? If not, move past the motions and sit down and talk to Jesus. Begin a real *relationship* with him today.

Maybe you have had a relationship with Jesus for some time. You know what it's like to have God live your days with you, helping you, whispering to you, comforting you, and nudging you in new directions. But in recent days, you've lost the connection with God. You're so busy, so behind in every area of your life, so needed by your kids, you can barely hear yourself think, much less hear any whispers God might be throwing your way. It's one more area of guilt—you haven't made the time and space for God that you think you should, but life rushes on, and you don't know what to do about it.

Stop, and Breathe

Now whatever your situation, Mom, stop. Whether you are just cracking yourself open to let Jesus in, or you're realizing that you need to begin a real relationship with him, or you need to find a way to get back to that relationship with him. Let's stop, and breathe. *Jesus, come now. Give my spirit some quiet. Show me how to live my days in relationship with you.*

Let's consider some areas that might help that to happen:

Quiet Yourself

Admittedly, that's easier said than done. The only guaranteed quiet is at night, sometimes only late at night. And that's when I'm nodding off, you say. Ask Jesus to help you find one part of your day when you can be quiet with him for just a few minutes. Maybe ten minutes before lying down to sleep. Maybe ten minutes when you first open your eyes in bed in the morning. Maybe a few minutes after the baby goes down for a nap. Maybe some minutes during a coffee break at work. Maybe while your husband puts the kids to bed.

Take those moments and sit with Jesus. Read a few verses in the Bible. Or find a devotional book that you like and read a little. Or write a short prayer in a journal. Don't worry about complete sentences or even making sense—just get your thoughts out. Make it a time when you are conscious of Jesus being with you, letting him love you and knowing he is hearing anything you want to say.

The important part is being quiet and knowing you're connecting with Jesus. He says in the Bible, "Come to me all you who are weary and burdened and I will give you rest" (Matthew 11:28). Keri Wyatt Kent wrote a book called *Breathe: Creating Space for God in a Hectic Life*. She says, "We live in a culture focused on doing. That's one reason so many of us wrestle with being a parent: time with our kids doesn't seem like we are producing anything. To ruthlessly eliminate hurry would make us feel 'unproductive.' ... But what if time that seems 'unproductive' actually isn't? I mean time when we focus on simply being with God, or just being—couldn't that 'produce' some things in our life, like peace and joy?"[2] Yes, that's just what Jesus is talking about when he tells us to come, he will give us rest.

An important part of that rest for us moms may be taking all those thoughts that are whirling around in our heads—"Am I handling Micah's tantrums the right way?" "Can we afford a bigger car?" "Can I handle continuing to work at home after this second child is born?" "How do I ask my mom to stop giving the kids so much candy and junk?"—and uttering them to God. God tells us in the Bible, "Do not be anxious about anything, but in everything, by prayer and petition, with thanksgiving, present your requests to God. And the peace of God, which transcends all understanding, will guard your hearts and your minds in Christ Jesus" (Philippians 4:6–7).

After you've spoken your concerns, stay quiet in order to hear how God may be speaking in response. He may speak from his Spirit to yours, and you'll just know he's talking. He may speak to your situation through the verses in the Bible you are reading. Or he may speak later on through a person in your life, as we discuss below. Quiet is important in giving us, and God, a time and a space to speak and to love.

If we can steal those few minutes away from all the other to-dos, we'll find that the time with Jesus will change the color of our days.

Relate

Jesus connects with us spiritually. He speaks to us and lives with us in ways that transcend audible language and physical presence. But he also knew that we would need him to be audible and physically present at times, so he arranged a way for that to happen after he physically left this earth. God put his Spirit—the Holy Spirit—into each of his followers so that we can "be" Jesus to one another.

That makes our relationship with other Jesus followers really important! We need Jesus and time with him, and we also need people in our lives who are walking with him and who can hug us and hear us and laugh and cry with us. We

What Every MOM Needs

need friends who have lived with him longer and can help point the way. We need other moms who are living with Jesus in much the same ways as we are. We need other parents who can help us raise our kids to know Jesus for themselves. We need other married couples who can help us make Jesus a living presence in our marriage.

If you don't have these kinds of friends, ask him to help you begin making some — like at church or in a MOPS group, for example. If you do have them, make time with them a priority.

Learn

No matter how much you do or don't know about God and life with him, you will draw closer to Jesus by continuing to learn. The Bible is an important way to do it. The Bible describes Jesus as "the Word" made flesh, expressing the vital presence of Jesus that comes to us through his words in the Bible. In living with Jesus we need to learn from the Bible and let him speak to us through it often. If you don't know the Bible, use a book that helps you get into the Bible and understand it better. (You can check out some suggestions in the resources at the end of this chapter.)

If you're just getting to know the Bible, get to know Jesus through one of the gospels: Matthew, Mark, Luke, or John. We can all appreciate the Psalms as we mother our children and experience many of the same emotions David did as he wrote these songs. The smaller books of the New Testament, like Galatians, Ephesians, Philippians, and Colossians are short but packed with promises and encouragement from God that we can hold on to in our day-to-day ups and downs.

As you grow as a follower of Jesus, you will want to study the Bible too. Studying the Bible is different from daily devotional reading. Studying involves coming to understand larger portions of the Bible as they relate to our life and existence. It teaches us important foundational information about God and what it means to be in relationship with him. If you aren't doing it, look for a way to make Bible study a part of your life.

Worship

There is nothing more freeing than getting our minds off ourselves and looking to God in worship. Worship can happen anywhere—in the bathroom while blow-drying our hair, on a walk with the Baby Bjorn strapped around us and the stroller in front of us, in the car when we're caught in traffic, or while we do the dishes—for the sixth time today. A special kind of worship also happens when we're with others who love Jesus, usually in a church. Church can become a real source of support for us as we try to live daily with Jesus. Even those "motions" can take on real meaning if we are doing them as another way of connecting with God.

If you have a church, are there ways you could enter more fully into a life of worship, or learning, or support with others there? Church is a good place to get involved in study of the Bible and in getting Jesus-centered support in mothering, parenting, womanhood, marriage, divorce recovery, and many other areas. If you don't have a church, visit one. If you don't like it, visit another. Look for one that holds closely to the Bible. Give it a little time and ask Jesus to help you find one that is right for you.

What Every **MOM** Needs

Serve

Sounds like a to-do at first, doesn't it? When we're in a relationship with Jesus, we'll find that we *want* to give back to him and to his work in our world. Sometimes that means helping out at church, volunteering, ushering, even teaching. Sometimes that means spending time with people who don't have what we have, giving away our children's toys, or encouraging someone who's sick or on bed rest during pregnancy. It can mean contributing financially to a Christian organization to address the HIV pandemic or help babies in China who need to be adopted.

Serving is giving back to Jesus as a gesture of love for all he has given us. It's not necessary to have a relationship with Jesus, but it does deepen our love for him.

Hope for Each Day, Each Challenge

When we look back through this book, chapter by chapter, and revisit all of the things we want as moms in the light of a relationship with Jesus, we can see that he does light the way in each area of need. Let's look at them, one by one:

- ✳ *Identity: I Want to Find "Me" Again.* God made each of us to fill a special purpose in this world. God wants us to find and be "me" more than we do, because he's made us and gifted us just the way we are for a reason.
- ✳ *Growth: I Want the Space to Develop "Me."* God has made each of us with unique potential, specific gifts, and a personhood that are a copy of no one else. We've each developed some of that potential, and the rest develops through a relationship with Jesus. Only in knowing him

and letting him continue forming us will we become all God intended us to be. With Jesus, growth like we've never imagined can happen.

* *Relationship: I Want Someone to Understand Me.* We need relationship — connection with people, regularly. People will never meet our needs completely, though. And every relationship will have its difficulties. Only a relationship with Jesus will completely satisfy us. And only a connection with him will enable us to carry on in all our other relationships.

* *Help: I Want Some Help!* God created us for community, to be dependent and not independent. In this state of need for others, we see our need for him. Help, really, comes from God. All the people in our life are given to us by him. And he is our ultimate Helper. He helps our spirits to find peace and rest. We can manage anything as moms with that kind of help.

* *Perspective: I Want to Focus on What Matters.* Perspective means developing a God-view of life. Jesus is our North Star — when life seems crazy and we're not sure about the right way to move forward, keeping our eyes on him allows the rest to fall into place. Jesus holds all that we are and all that we want to be and do, bringing hope to life.

Hold on to Hope, Hold on to Jesus

Moms, whether you are just getting to know Jesus or are turning a corner with him as you try to navigate life as a mother of young children, the hope you can find in him is *real.* No other person, no amount of money, no gargantuan effort, no megadose of "me" time, and no super-duper organizational system will come close to being in your life what Jesus can be for you. We need this reminder again and again, no matter how long we've known him.

One longtime Christian expresses this very truth. Larry Crabb, a psychologist and follower of Jesus, writes, "Brokenness is realizing he is all we have. Hope is realizing he is all we need. Joy is realizing he is all we want.... I have spent so much of my life hearing that sort of teaching and thinking of it as true but not immediately necessary to grasp. I now see it differently. I am beginning to understand that the loneliness I have for so long tried to relieve by marrying, by developing friendships, by writing books, by thinking of funny things to say at parties, is really a hunger for God."[3]

We need to hold on to Jesus and satisfy *all* of our hunger in him. Remember this when life gets busy and you begin running a mile a minute and the empty feeling starts to set in again. "I want this ... and this ... and this ..." *I want you, Jesus. Fill me. Show me. Help me. Guide me.*

Hold on to Jesus and he will hold on to you. He says so with these beautiful words: "He tends his flock like a shepherd: He gathers the lambs [your children!] in his arms and carries them close to his heart; he gently leads those [you!] that have young" (Isaiah 40:11).

Words for Inspiration and Understanding

Here are some quotes about our need for God and a relationship with him through his Son, Jesus:

You have made us for yourself, O God, and our hearts are restless till they find rest in you.

—Augustine, *Confessions*

Man searches in vain, but finds nothing to help him, other than to see an infinite emptiness that can only be filled by One who is infinite and unchanging. In other words, it can only be filled by God himself.

—Blaise Pascal

The soul hardly ever realizes it, but whether he is a believer or not, his loneliness is really a homesickness for God.

—Hubert Van Zeller, *We Die Standing Up*

Our problem is not so much that God doesn't give us what we hope for as it is that we don't know the right thing for which to hope.... Hope is not what you expect.

—Max Lucado, *God Came Near*

From the Bible:

This is love: not that we loved God, but that he loved us and sent his Son as an atoning sacrifice [satisfactory payment] for our sins.

—1 John 4:10

What Every **MOM** Needs

Hope deferred makes the heart sick, but a longing fulfilled is a tree of life.

—Proverbs 13:12

Now faith is being sure of what we hope for and certain of what we do not see.

—Hebrews 11:1

And my God will meet all your needs according to his glorious riches in Christ Jesus.

—Philippians 4:19

For I am convinced that neither death nor life, neither angels nor demons, neither the present nor the future, nor any powers, neither height nor depth, nor anything else in all creation, will be able to separate us from the love of God that is in Christ Jesus our Lord.

—Romans 8:38–39

Mom Me Time

Mom Me Time 1
I Just Can't Do the "Jesus Thing"

Before you walk away from Jesus, let's take a look at why you're feeling what you are. Read the voices of other moms below. Do your feelings resemble any of these?

* I grew up in a religious home and community that considered our religion a given part of life. But as I grew, I began to see a lot of ugly stuff underneath all the posturing. There is no way I would ever go back to that religion.

* I was very hurt by someone who claimed to be a Christian. I don't trust Christians, and I'm not sure believing all this stuff really makes a difference in a person.

* Come on. Anyone who has got an education knows that there are too many holes in the Bible and in the story of Jesus. I'm not going to exchange my brain for some feelings-oriented faith.

* I know enough about the pain in this world to know that if God was really good, he would surely do something about all the horrible things that happen.

* I've looked out for myself since I was a tiny kid. I'm not one to ask for help or let someone else manage my life. To me, I guess it seems that this Jesus stuff is for wimps.

* My mom considered herself a Christian and always told me I needed to "get right with God." I told her I'd never be dealing with God, if there is one, and I'm not going to change my mind.

If any of these voices suggest a story similar to yours, will you pray one prayer?

Jesus, if you are there, and if there is something better for my life, show me.

Now just watch and wait.

Mom Me Time 2

Give Me a Boost!

Does your life with Jesus need help? Do you feel like, rather than a "vita-boost" or a "protein boost," you need a "Jesus boost"? Do you need some help in getting growing and relating with him again? Consider one of these approaches:

* *Start a prayer journal.* Any notebook will do. Make two columns. Pray every day, jotting down prayer needs in one column and ways you see God answering in the other column. It's a great way to watch God working in your life!

* *Start a contemplative prayer group with a friend.* Contemplative prayer involves sitting in the quiet with God and focusing on a verse in the Bible or a short prayer. As you sit and quietly reflect, let God speak to you as he chooses.

* *If you're married, read the Bible or a book on spiritual growth with your husband.* Spend a little time at night or in the morning reading and talking together. He can become your closest partner in spiritual growth.

* *Find a spiritual mentor.* Do you know someone who might agree to mentor you, or walk with you as a friend and guide both as you mother and grow closer to Jesus? Maybe someone at church or someone you have met in the past? Pray about it and then approach this person.

* *Join a Bible study.* There's so much to learn about God's Word, the Bible. Tackling one book of the Bible at a time, with friends who are perhaps further along in

their faith journey, is a great way to gain understanding of God's intended design for our days.

* *Volunteer!* Let God stretch you and teach you as you focus on helping others. Keep your ear out for opportunities, and ask God to show you how he wants to use you.

* *Simplify!* Maybe you've been *doing* too much. Can you pull out of some volunteering? Slow down with your kids? Choose to work fewer hours at home? Give yourself more downtime? Use this time to be with God and listen for his voice.

Mom Me Time 3
Really Dark Days

Do you know Jesus but can't see him or feel him or hear him right now? And it seems you've felt this way for days, or weeks, or months? Are you experiencing what one man, St. John of the Cross, centuries ago called a "dark night of the soul"?

Sometimes Christians go through periods when it seems God has left us. We pray and don't hear any response. We ask and feel we get nothing. We reach and feel like no one is reaching back. Is God there? Does he see my life and hear my cries? We cry for help, but we get no response.

Emilie Griffin writes, "Darkness is one foot in front of another.... It is doing what comes to hand without feeling or seeing the grace by which it is to be done. Do you remember, when we were children, how we could not feel ourselves growing? The change in us could not be sensed until someone else insisted we had become taller and measured us against himself. Darkness, then, is that growth that comes in silence and by remaining perfectly still....

"The goal, in darkness, is not to whimper about it, but to live it, while it lasts, as deeply as any other gift God gives us in experience. One day, without knowing how or why, something has lifted. The darkness has simply gone away."[4]

Mom Me Time 4

In a World Like This, Is There Hope for My Kids?

Everywhere we look, we see monsters in our culture that seem to be just waiting to pounce on our tiny ones when they're a bit older and eat them up. Drugs and alcohol. Pornography on the Internet. Child molestation at kids' groups and by individuals who might be living right down the street. Gambling. A culture that idolizes money. Skyrocketing personal and national debt. Pollution in the air, the water, and our food. A media culture that captures children's time and allegiance. The list goes on ...

Is there hope? Where do we begin as moms to keep our kids safe and steer them past these scary realities? How do we help them encounter Jesus for themselves and want his life rather than all the counterfeits out there?

Pray

It's the biggest thing we can do for our children. Theologian Karl Barth said, "To clasp the hands in prayer is the beginning of an uprising against the disorder of the world." When we pray we join with the God of the universe who has infinitely more power than anything the world could throw at our children.

In their book *Praying the Bible for Your Children*, David and Heather Kopp say, "Prayer is a God-given part of our urge to protect, care for, and shape the offspring He has given us. Yet we don't pray just to accomplish our parental goals; we pray to grow in wisdom ourselves, to recover, to hold on. And we pray to give thanks. 'Children are a gift from God; they are his reward.' ... And ultimately this is why we pray: because knowing God and His love is our greatest treasure. We see it shining like a million stars all around. Life is hard, but our treasure is true, and we want to pass it on to our children."[5]

Influence

As parents we are in first position to make great use of the power of prayer for our children. Because we know them best and care the most, we can pray fervently and with genuine insight. Other influences—good and bad—may prevail in our children's lives for a while, but they never come first or last longest. As someone so aptly said, "A mother is the first book read and the last put aside in every child's library."

Surround

Make sure your kids have lots of other Christians in their lives, both young and old, who spend time with them, love them, and become models to them. Marlene LeFever calls this building a "dream team" for your kids: "Young children are hero worshipers and parents are typically the biggest heroes of all; they can do no wrong. But all that changes around fifth or sixth grade. Suddenly children see their parents' flaws, and for a few years they want to be as different from their parents as possible. That's where the 'second string' comes in. A few well-placed Christian adults can provide the guidance and support your child is hesitant to accept from you."[6] She suggests Sunday school teachers, Christian neighbors — some of whom may become surrogate grandparents — contact with faraway relatives through e-mail and phone, your church family, and your pastor as great people to see often with your kids.

We can't protect our kids completely, but we can do a lot toward putting them in the hands of God, who can. No matter what our kids encounter as they grow, we *can* hold on to hope as moms, because we can hold on to a God who is bigger than any monster out there.

Mom We Time

1. Have you had a day like Kylah, at the beginning of this chapter, where you realized that you needed hope that comes from somewhere outside yourself? Talk together about when this has happened for you.

2. Did you turn to God? If you know Jesus, what kind of a difference has relationship with him made? What do you do on the hard days?

3. God intends for us to be his arms and his ears for one another. As moms, we need to experience the love of Jesus through each other. Partner with another mom or two and tell them one thing in your life that threatens your sense of hope. Maybe it's your sink full of dirty dishes. Maybe it's your child's sassy mouth, and she's only four! Maybe it's a hard place in your marriage. Or maybe a concern you have about your job or your work at home.

If you're comfortable, first put your arms around each other in a big mom hug—we need the power of touch with one another. Then use your ears to care for each other. Tell about where you need hope, and encourage your partner in the area where she needs hope.

For Further Reading

Books

For Questions about Faith or Jesus

Lewis, C. S. *Mere Christianity.*
McDowell, Josh. *More Than a Carpenter.*
Strobel, Lee. *The Case for Christ: A Journalist's Personal Investigation of the Evidence of Jesus.*
———. *The Case for Faith: A Journalist Investigates the Toughest Objections to Christianity.*

What Every **MOM** Needs

Yancey, Philip. *The Jesus I Never Knew.*

Zacharias, Ravi. *Can Man Live without God?*

For Developing a Relationship with Jesus

Blackaby, Henry T., and Claude V. King. *Experiencing God: Knowing and Doing His Will.*

Hybels, Bill. *Honest to God? Becoming an Authentic Christian.*

Lawrence, Brother. *Practicing the Presence of God.*

Lucado, Max. *No Wonder They Call Him Savior.*

Mom's Devotional Bible (New International Version).

MOPS International, *Mommy Dreams.*

———. *The Gift of Hope for Moms.*

Morgan, Elisa. *God's Words of Life for Moms.*

———. *The Orchard: A Parable.*

Tozer, A. W. *Pursuit of God.*

Warren, Rick. *The Purpose Driven Life: What on Earth Am I Here For?.*

Yancey, Philip. *Prayer: Does It Matter?*

Yancey, Philip, and Brenda Quinn. *Meet the Bible: A Panorama of God's Word in 366 Daily Readings and Reflections.*

For Continued Growth in Jesus

Chambers, Oswald. *My Utmost for His Highest.*

Craker, Lorilee. *Just Give Me a Little Piece of Quiet: Sixty Mini-retreats for a Mom's Soul.*

Foster, Richard. *Celebration of Discipline: The Path to Spiritual Growth.*

Kent, Keri Wyatt. *Breathe: Creating Space for God in a Hectic Life.*

Kroeker, Ann. *The Contemplative Mom: Restoring Rich Relationship with God in the Midst of Motherhood.*

Morgan, Elisa. *Naked Fruit: Getting Honest about the Fruit of the Spirit.*

———. *Twinkle: Sharing Your Faith One Light at a Time.*

Omartian, Stormie. *The Power of a Praying Parent.*

———. *The Power of a Praying Wife.*

Websites

www.journeyofjoy.com. Offers a simple, clear explanation of the hope that can be found in a relationship with Jesus.

About MOPS

It was a Tuesday morning at about 9:30. They had each faced spilled cereal, tangled hair, and a few had even been forced to change their outfits due to last-minute baby spit-up on a shoulder or lap. They had driven, or walked with strollers, to the church and dropped off their little ones in the nursery. They had made it!

And now they sat, knees almost touching in the circle of children's chairs from the Sunday school room. Hands held cups of hot coffee and doughnuts in utter freedom, because this treat did not have to be shared with the sticky fingers of a child. Mouths moved in eager, uninterrupted conversation. Eyes sparkled with enthusiasm. Hearts stirred with understanding. Needs were met.

That morning, back in 1973, was the first morning of MOPS. From its humble beginning in a church in Wheat Ridge, Colorado, with a handful of moms, MOPS International now supports MOPS groups in almost 4,500 locations in all fifty of the United States and in thirty-five other countries.

Some 120,000 moms are touched by local MOPS groups, and many, many more are encouraged through the communication arms of MOPS: *MOMSense* magazine and radio broadcast, an active website at www.MOPS.org, *Connections Leadership* magazine, and books such as this.

MOPS groups are chartered ministries of local churches and meet at a variety of times and locations: daytime, evenings, and on weekends; in churches, homes, and workplaces.

Today when a mom enters a MOPS meeting, she'll be greeted by a friendly face and escorted to the MOPPETS program, where she leaves her children during the MOPS program. In MOPPETS, children from infancy through kindergarten experience a safe and caring environment while being introduced to crafts, songs, and learning opportunities. For many families, this is the first or only opportunity for children to enjoy making new friends and learning about God.

Once her children are settled, the MOPS mom joins a program tailor-made to meet her needs. She can grab something good to eat and not have to share it! She can finish a sentence and not have to speak in Children-ese!

The program begins with a brief lesson taught by a MOPS mentor (an older mom who's been through the challenging early years of mothering and who can share from her experience and from the truths taught in the Bible), or a speaker from the community. Then the women break into small discussion groups where there are no "wrong answers" and women are free to share their joys and struggles with other moms who truly understand their feelings. In these moments, long-lasting friendships are often made on the common ground of finally being understood.

The women then participate in a creative activity. For moms who are often frustrated by the impossibility of completing anything in their unpredictable days, this time is deeply satisfying. It provides a sense of accomplishment and growth for many moms, as well as the chance for casual conversation.

Since moms of preschoolers themselves lead MOPS groups, the program offers women a chance to develop their leadership skills and other latent talents. It takes organization, up-front abilities, financial management, creativity, and relational skills to run a MOPS program successfully.

The MOPS meeting helps moms feel refreshed and better able to mother. MOPS recognizes that moms have needs too! And when we learn to take the time to meet our own needs, we find we are more effective in meeting the needs of our families. This is how one mom described MOPS:

> MOPS means I am able to share the joys, frustrations, and insecurities of being a mom. Our meetings provide the opportunity to hear someone else say, "I was up all night," or "They're driving me crazy!" or "He doesn't understand." While listening to others I may discover a fresh idea or a new perspective that helps me tackle the job of parenting, home management, or being a good wife. It's important to feel normal and not alone. Burdens are lifted when the woman next to me says, "I know exactly how you feel." MOPS is a place for my children to interact with peers while I savor some uninterrupted conversation. I was not a Christian when I began attending MOPS. Over the past year I have experienced tremendous spiritual growth, and I know that MOPS was a contributor to that growth. Now fellowship with other Christian women is an integral reason for me to attend. I thank the Lord for bringing me and my children to MOPS.
>
> —A MOPS woman from Porterville, California

The MOPS program also enables moms to reach out and help other moms, fulfilling not only a need to belong and be understood, but a need to help others. Here are some examples:

* I attended a MOPS group only two times before my baby was hospitalized with a critical illness. Women from this MOPS group provided meals, cleaned my house, even employed my teenaged daughter as a babysitter to keep her occupied while my baby was hospitalized for fifty days. I felt overwhelmed by this kind of outreach from moms who hardly knew me. My baby is recovering, and I will forever be changed myself.

* My MOPS group has become my extended family. Some of the women have watched my boys when I needed to go somewhere or do something without the boys. I have come to depend upon them, and this means a lot to me. I hope they feel like they can depend on me too.

To find out if there is a MOPS group near you, or to tap into the resources of MOPS, please visit the MOPS International website at www.MOPS.org. Phone us at (303) 733-5353. Or e-mail info@MOPS.org. To learn how to start a MOPS group in your community, call (888) 910-6677.

Notes

Introduction

1. Lawrence J. Crabb, *Basic Principles of Biblical Counseling* (Grand Rapids, MI: Zondervan, 1975), 53.
2. Sigmund Freud, *Outline of Psychoanalysis SE 23* (London: Hogarth, 1940), 32.

Chapter 1: Identity

1. Nancy Stafford, *Beauty by the Book: Seeing Yourself as God Sees You* (Sisters, OR: Multnomah, 2002), 232.
2. Erik Fromm, *The Art of Living* (New York: Harper and Row, 1956), 43.
3. Stafford, *Beauty by the Book*, 233.
4. Ibid., 159.
5. Martha Thatcher, "The Most Difficult Love," *Discipleship Journal* 35 (1986), 19.
6. Cecil Osborne, *The Art of Learning to Love Yourself* (Grand Rapids, MI: Zondervan, 1976), 38.
7. Philip Yancey, *What's So Amazing about Grace?* (Grand Rapids, MI: Zondervan, 1997), 71.
8. Tracey Bianchi, "Should I Keep Going?" *Connections Leadership Magazine* 4 (2006): 4–5.
9. Excerpted and adapted from Florence Littauer, *After Every Wedding Comes a Marriage* (Eugene, OR: Harvest House, 1981), and Marita Littauer and Florence Littauer, *Wired That Way* (Ventura, CA: Gospel Light, 2006). Used by permission. Not to be duplicated. Additional copies may be ordered by calling (800) 433-6633 or visiting www.thepersonalities.com.
10. Judith Couchman, *Designing a Woman's Life Study Guide: A Bible Study and Workbook* (Sisters, OR: Multnomah, 1996), 39. Excerpted from *Designing a Woman's Life Bible Study and Workbook* © 1996 by Judy C. Couchman. Used by permission of Multnomah Publishers Inc.

11. Ibid., 40. Used by permission.
12. Ibid., 49. Used by permission.
13. Richard J. Foster, *Prayers from the Heart* (San Francisco: HarperSanFrancisco, 1994), 54.
14. John Eldredge and Stasi Eldredge, *Captivating: Unveiling the Mystery of a Woman's Soul* (Nashville: Nelson, 2005), 216.

Chapter 2: Growth

1. Katherine Ellison, *The Mommy Brain: How Motherhood Makes Us Smarter* (New York: Basic, 2005), 3.
2. Dale Hanson Bourke, "What Motherhood Really Means," *Everyday Miracles* (Dallas: Word, 1989), 2.
3. Judith Couchman, *Designing a Woman's Life: Discovering Your Unique Purpose and Passion* (Sisters, OR: Multnomah, 1996), 88. Excerpted from *Designing a Woman's Life* © 1996 by Judy C. Couchman. Used by permission of Multnomah Publishers Inc.
4. Katrina Kenison, *Mitten Strings for God: Reflections for Mothers in a Hurry* (New York: Warner, 2000), 200.
5. Ellison, *The Mommy Brain*, 9.
6. Deena Lee Wilson, *A Mom's Legacy: Five Simple Ways to Say Yes to What Counts Forever* (Ventura, CA: Regal, 1999), 136.
7. Ibid., 134.
8. Henry Cloud and John Townsend, *How People Grow: What the Bible Reveals about Personal Growth* (Grand Rapids, MI: Zondervan, 2001), 29.
9. John Eldredge and Stasi Eldredge, *Captivating: Unveiling the Mystery of a Woman's Soul* (Nashville: Nelson, 2005), 145.
10. Ted Engstrom, *The Pursuit of Excellence* (Grand Rapids, MI: Zondervan, 1982), 17.
11. Gary Hardaway, "When Dreams Die," *Moody Monthly* (June 1986), 20.
12. Barbara Sher, with Annie Gottlieb, *Wishcraft* (New York: Ballantine, 1979), 5.
13. Couchman, *Designing a Woman's Life*, 70. Used by permission.
14. Dottie McDowell, "Dottie's Delight Article," in Dave Ray, *Mom's Check-Up* (Royal Oak, MI: Core Ministries, 1994), 11. Used by permission.
15. Adapted from Couchman, *Designing a Woman's Life*, 69. Used by permission.
16. Adapted from Cindy Tolliver, *At-Home Motherhood* (San Jose, CA: Resource Publications, 1994), 150–52.

17. Adapted material by Eric Swanson for Campus Crusade for Christ (unpublished).
18. Helen Ferris, ed., *Favorite Poems Old and New* (Garden City, NY: Doubleday, 1957), 22.

Chapter 3: Relationship

1. Marla Paul, *The Friendship Crisis: Finding, Making, and Keeping Friends When You're Not a Kid Anymore* (New York: Rodale, 2004), 7.
2. Larry Crabb, *Connecting: Healing for Ourselves and Our Relationships* (Nashville: Word, 1997), 38, 45.
3. Laura Jensen Walker, *Girl Time: A Celebration of Chick Flicks, Bad Hair Days and Good Friends* (Grand Rapids, MI: Revell, 2004), 137.
4. Paul, *The Friendship Crisis*, 14.
5. *Rocky Mountain News* (April 7, 1985).
6. Sharon Hersh, *Bravehearts: Unlocking the Courage to Love with Abandon* (Colorado Springs: Waterbrook, 2000), 51–52.
7. Walter Wangerin Jr., "You Are, You Are, You Are," *Lutheran Journal* (January 24, 1990), 5.
8. Ibid., 10.
9. Elizabeth Cody Newenhuyse, "Friendship Fizzle," *Today's Christian Woman* (January/February 1995), 51.
10. Lorilee Craker, *We Should Do This More Often* (Colorado Springs: Waterbrook, 2005), 144. Reprinted from *We Should Do This More Often*. Copyright © 2005 by Lorilee Craker. Used by permission of WaterBrook Press, Colorado Springs, CO. All rights reserved.
11. Dale Hanson Bourke, *Everyday Miracles: What Motherhood Really Means* (Dallas: Word, 1989), 4.
12. Drs. Les and Leslie Parrott, quoted in Craker, *We Should Do This More Often*, 2–3. Reprinted from *We Should Do This More Often*. Copyright © 2005 by Lorilee Craker. Used by permission of WaterBrook Press, Colorado Springs, CO. All rights reserved.
13. Ibid., 23.
14. Ibid., 78–79.
15. "When Sex Hurts," *Today's Christian Woman* (November/December 2004), 62. Also, www.christianitytoday.com/tcw/2004/006/13.62.html.
16. Paul Tournier, *To Understand Each Other* (Atlanta: John Knox, 1967), 29–30.

17. Reprinted and adapted from Cindy Tolliver, *At-Home Motherhood* (San Jose, CA: Resource Publications, 1994), 40–41.
18. Sister Basilea Schink, *The Hidden Treasure in Suffering* (Lakeland, MI: Marshall, Morgan, and Scott, 1985), 35–36.

Chapter 4: Help

1. Carla Barnhill, *The Myth of the Perfect Mother* (Grand Rapids, MI: Baker, 2004), 98.
2. Donna Partow, *No More Lone Ranger Moms* (Bloomington, MN: Bethany, 1995), 13.
3. Marla Paul, *The Friendship Crisis: Finding, Making, and Keeping Friends When You're Not a Kid Anymore* (New York: Rodale, 2004), 167–68.
4. Karol Ladd and Jane Jarrell, *The Frazzled Factor: Relief for Working Moms* (Nashville: W, 2005), 47.
5. Ruth Barton, *Becoming a Woman of Strength* (Wheaton, IL: Shaw, 1994), 193, 205.
6. Mary Stewart Van Leeuwen, *Gender and Grace* (Downers Grove, IL: InterVarsity, 1990), 157–58, 266.
7. Barnhill, *Myth of the Perfect Mother*, 67.
8. Ibid.
9. Ibid., 68.
10. Ladd and Jarrell, *Frazzled Factor*, 104–5.
11. Cathy Penshorn, *Juggling Tasks, Tots, and Time* (Grand Rapids, MI: Zondervan, 2001), 62–70.
12. Patricia Sprinkle, *Do I Have To?* (Grand Rapids, MI: Zondervan, 1993), 87. Taken from *Do I Have To?* by Patricia Sprinkle. Copyright © 1993 by Patricia Sprinkle. Used by permission of the Zondervan Corporation.
13. Ibid., 106–7.
14. Ibid., 80.
15. Adapted from Dave Ray, *Mom's Check-Up* (Royal Oak, MI: Core Ministries, 1994), 52. Used by permission.
16. Ibid., 67.

Chapter 5: Perspective

1. Annie Dillard, in Timothy K. Jones, "Death in the Mirror," *Christianity Today* (June 24, 1991), 31.
2. John Eldredge and Stasi Eldredge, *Captivating: Unveiling the Mystery of a Woman's Soul* (Nashville: Nelson, 2005), 48–49.

3. Marianne Neifert, in Betty Johnson, "The Juggling Act of Dr. Mom," *Virtue* (March/April 1994), 39.

4. Charles R. Swindoll, *The Strong Family* (Grand Rapids, MI: Zondervan, 1991), 155.

5. Elizabeth Phillips Runkle, *Monmouth, the Key* (Fall 1994), 13.

6. Debbie Barr, *A Season at Home* (Grand Rapids, MI: Zondervan, 1993), 26.

7. Joy Jacobs, "Mysteries of Motherhood," *Christian Herald* (May 1986), 22.

8. Max Lucado, *God Came Near* (Portland, OR: Multnomah, 1987), 160.

9. Kathy Fictorie, "If You Give a Mom a Muffin," *MomSense* (August/September 2002), 22.

10. Jane Jarrell, *Secrets of a Mid-Life Mom* (Colorado Springs: NavPress, 2004), 154.

11. Carla Barnhill, *The Myth of the Perfect Mother* (Grand Rapids, MI: Baker, 2004), 84, 95–96.

Chapter 6: Hope

1. Philip Yancey, *What's So Amazing about Grace?* (Grand Rapids, MI: Zondervan, 1997), 45.

2. Keri Wyatt Kent, *Breathe: Creating Space for God in a Hectic Life* (Grand Rapids, MI: Revell, 2005), 45.

3. Larry Crabb, *The Safest Place on Earth* (Nashville: Word, 1999), 39.

4. Emilie Griffin, *Clinging: The Experience of Prayer* (New York: McKracken, 1983, 1994), 40–41.

5. David Kopp and Heather Kopp, *Praying the Bible for Your Children* (Colorado Springs: Waterbrook, 1997), 5.

6. Marlene LeFever, "Building a Dream Team," *Christian Parenting Today* (Winter 2003), 26.

MOTHERS OF

M♥PS.

PRESCHOOLERS

MOPS International
Membership Program

Being a member of MOPS International encourages, equips, and develops every mother of a preschooler to realize her potential as a woman, mother, and leader.

Ongoing MOPS International benefits will encourage you throughout the entire year!

Annual MOPS International Membership benefits include:

- *MOMSense* magazine subscription (bi-monthly)
- Membership card (special *members only* pricing on MOPS products and events)
- Children's DVD (December)
- Mom book (May)
- Weekly MOM-E-Mails
- Parenting resources at the www.MOPShop.org
- Events: parenting and leadership training
- MOPS website at www.MOPS.org

How do I become a member of MOPS International?

For only $20 you will receive a year's worth of the *encouragement*, *training*, and *development* every mother of a preschooler needs!

Visit us today: **www.MOPS.org/MOMSenseoffer**

Real Moms

Exploding the Myths of Motherhood

*Elisa Morgan and
Carol Kuykendall*

Mom! Get Real . . . and Get Free!

Are you tired of constantly trying—and failing—to be a perfect mom? Stop beating yourself up and let the truth about motherhood set you free! *Real Moms* debunks the "good mom" fallacies that have weighed you down by giving you some liberating "real mom" truths. This book punctures such mothering myths as:

- Good moms look good all the time.
- Good moms keep everybody happy.
- Good moms instinctively know what their children need.
- Good moms take responsibility for how their children turn out.
- Good moms don't admit their feelings of guilt or anger or fear, because to admit those feelings might make them look like they are not good moms.

Each chapter examines a myth and its corresponding reality, and ends with a how-to practical application, a "Real Mom" story, questions for reflection and discussion, and "Real Mom" quotes from real mothers.

Wouldn't you love to be free to accept your imperfections? Free not to feel guilty about your limitations? Free to ask for help, free to be real, free to grow? Freedom is in store for you—freedom to be the best mom you can be. This book will show you the way.

Softcover: 0-310-24703-9

Raising Great Kids Workbook for Parents of Teenagers

A Comprehensive Guide to Parenting with Grace and Truth

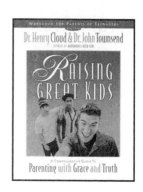

Dr. Henry Cloud and
Dr. John Townsend

When kids hit their teens, their character unfolds in increasingly consequential ways. Your job as a parent is far from done! During those stormy teenage years from ages 13 to 19, your child needs your help in developing traits that are vital to his or her future well-being: connection, responsibility, reality, competence, morality, and worship/spiritual life.

Based on *Raising Great Kids*, the *Raising Great Kids Workbook for Parents of Teenagers* is filled with self-tests, discussion material, exercises, and practical applications that can help you turn key concepts into a natural way of parenting. Look at it as your navigation guide for helping your son or daughter make the transition to adulthood safely and successfully.

What does it take to raise great kids? Conflicting opinions may leave you feeling confused. Get tough! Show acceptance. Lay down the rules. Lighten up, already. There's got to be a balance—and there is. Dr. Henry Cloud and Dr. John Townsend help you provide the care and acceptance that make grace real to your kids, and the firmness and discipline that give direction. At last, here is an effective middle ground for raising your children to handle life with maturity and wisdom.

Softcover: 0-310-23437-9

Children Change a Marriage

What Every Couple Needs to Know

*Elisa Morgan and
Carol Kuykendall*

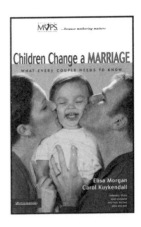

*We Interrupt This Marriage . . .
to Raise Children.*

Just when you thought you'd adjusted to each other—just when you and your spouse had achieved a satisfying balance in your relationship—it happened. Your first child arrived. Things have never been the same since . . . and they never will be. So how do you regain your equilibrium now that you have children?

Elisa Morgan and Carol Kuykendall of MOPS International (Mothers of Preschoolers) know your frustrations. And they know the answers. Not pretty theories, but honest, qualified insights and approaches that can help you turn the transitions of parenthood into times of transformation in your marriage.

Children Change a Marriage is for every husband and wife entering the adventure of parenthood. Read it, apply it, and look forward with hope. The best years of your life together lie ahead!

Softcover: 0-310-24299-1

Pick up a copy today at your favorite bookstore!

ZONDERVAN®

GRAND RAPIDS, MICHIGAN 49530 USA

WWW.ZONDERVAN.COM

Beyond Macaroni and Cheese

Edited by
Mary Beth Lagerborg
and Karen J. Parks

When the family has got to eat, and there's little time to prepare a meal, and the kids are picky eaters, and you've already exhausted the week's quota for macaroni and cheese, turn here. You'll find meals tasty and easy enough to coax you beyond the familiar, boxed standbys. These recipes were submitted and tested by moms in MOPS (Mothers of Preschoolers) groups across the country. Moms on the front lines, swapping recipes they know will work for families.

Softcover, Layflat: 0-310-21978-7

Pick up a copy today at your favorite bookstore!

ZONDERVAN®

GRAND RAPIDS, MICHIGAN 49530 USA

WWW.ZONDERVAN.COM

Life Interrupted

The Scoop on Being a Young Mom

Tricia Goyer

One day you're a typical student. You're working part-time at McDonald's to pay for your clothes and car. The next day, you're a mother-to-be. You're confused and scared. Emotional and standoffish. You feel like a kid, but now with a huge responsibility.

How could your life change so fast? Your youth wasn't supposed to be packed with worries and obligations, Lamaze classes and daycare choices—and you've still got work and school to deal with. Whatever happened to fun, friendships, and dating? You'd do anything for your baby—but what about you? What about your needs?

Sharing stories from her own experience as a teenage mom and from other young mothers, Tricia Goyer shows you what to do about meeting nine basic needs that all young moms have. Needs such as the need to be appreciated, the need to know your life is not at a dead end, and the need to be loved. In *Life Interrupted*, you'll meet lots of young moms just like you. You'll also meet God, who cares about you very much.

Softcover: 0-310-25316-0

Pick up a copy today at your favorite bookstore!

ZONDERVAN®

GRAND RAPIDS, MICHIGAN 49530 USA

WWW.ZONDERVAN.COM

The Birthday Book

Creative Ways to Celebrate Your Child's Special Day

Shelly Radic

It's More Than a Birthday!

It's a fantastic opportunity to affirm your child's unique, God-given abilities and interests. *The Birthday Book* shows you the priceless benefits of celebrating your child's birthday, then gives you a myriad of meaningful ways to make his or her special day fun and totally unforgettable.

From creating a keepsake videotape, to developing a dinnertime birthday tradition, to planning a parent-child birthday getaway or organizing a birthday bash for your child's friends, you'll find mom-tested strategies inside, together with a bonanza of ideas for themes, invitations, decorations, food, games, resources, and tips. Even better, it's all laid out in age groups to help you and your child celebrate in appropriate ways for every phase of the growing-up years:

- Fun When You're One
- Terrific Times for Twos and Threes
- Fun Festivities for Fours and Fives
- Stupendous Fun for School-Age Kids
- Totally Teens

Softcover: 0-310-24704-7

Pick up a copy today at your favorite bookstore!

GRAND RAPIDS, MICHIGAN 49530 USA

WWW.ZONDERVAN.COM

Ready for Kindergarten

An Award-Winning Teacher's Plan to Prepare Your Child for School

Sharon Wilkins

You are the most important teacher your child will ever have. Filled with 156 fun activities designed to equip boys and girls for school success, this unique little book can show you how to help your child lay the foundation for developing healthy friendships and a love for God. In addition, it can help you give your child a giant head start in such core subjects as math, reading, science, art, and music! Through three simple, creative activities per week, you can laugh and play with your child while teaching important skills. Let an award-winning kindergarten teacher with twenty-four years of classroom experience show how exciting activities—from making your initials out of Play Doh to building a cardboard train out of boxes—can make your child *Ready for Kindergarten*!

Softcover: 0-310-23659-2

Pick up a copy today at your favorite bookstore!

ZONDERVAN®

GRAND RAPIDS, MICHIGAN 49530 USA

WWW.ZONDERVAN.COM

Getting Out of Your Kids' Faces and into Their Hearts

Valerie Bell

"You can enjoy your kids more, relax around them, and love them better" is the fresh message Valerie Bell has for parents feeling overwhelmed by the responsibilities of raising children. Finally, here is a book that is not about how to manage, train, and discipline your children, but about how to have a relationship with them. *Getting Out of Your Kids' Faces and into Their Hearts* will guide you toward becoming a warm, nurturing parent.

Softcover: 0-310-48451-0

Pick up a copy today at your favorite bookstore!

ZONDERVAN®

GRAND RAPIDS, MICHIGAN 49530 USA

WWW.ZONDERVAN.COM

NIV Mom's Devotional Bible

Mom, you don't have to go it alone!

The *Mom's Devotional Bible* is designed to be a trusted source of wisdom to help you as you learn how to be the kind of mom God wants you to be. It offers a year of weekday and weekend devotions that are full of good advice and encouragement from Elisa Morgan, president of Mothers of Preschoolers International (MOPS). Her inspiring commentaries help you understand and delight in your vital role of raising children. You'll also find resources that show you where to turn for help with the special challenges you face, and that offer insight into your role as a mother. The *Mom's Devotional Bible* helps you be the very best mom you can be

Hardcover, Printed: 0-310-92501-0

Pick up a copy today at your favorite bookstore!

ZONDERVAN®

GRAND RAPIDS, MICHIGAN 49530 USA

WWW.ZONDERVAN.COM

God's Words of Life for Women

from the New International Version

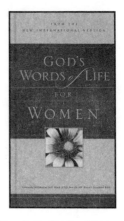

From the *NIV Women's Devotional Bible 2*, this topically arranged promise book includes Scripture verses and timely devotional thoughts. With contributions from Joni Eareckson Tada, Ruth Bell Graham, Emilie Barnes, Rosa Parks, Elizabeth Elliott, and other godly women, *God's Words of Life for Women* gives practical wisdom for your life. This beautiful book is perfect for personal use or to share with a friend.

Hardcover, Padded: 0-310-81320-4

Pick up a copy today at your favorite bookstore!

GRAND RAPIDS, MICHIGAN 49530 USA

WWW.ZONDERVAN.COM